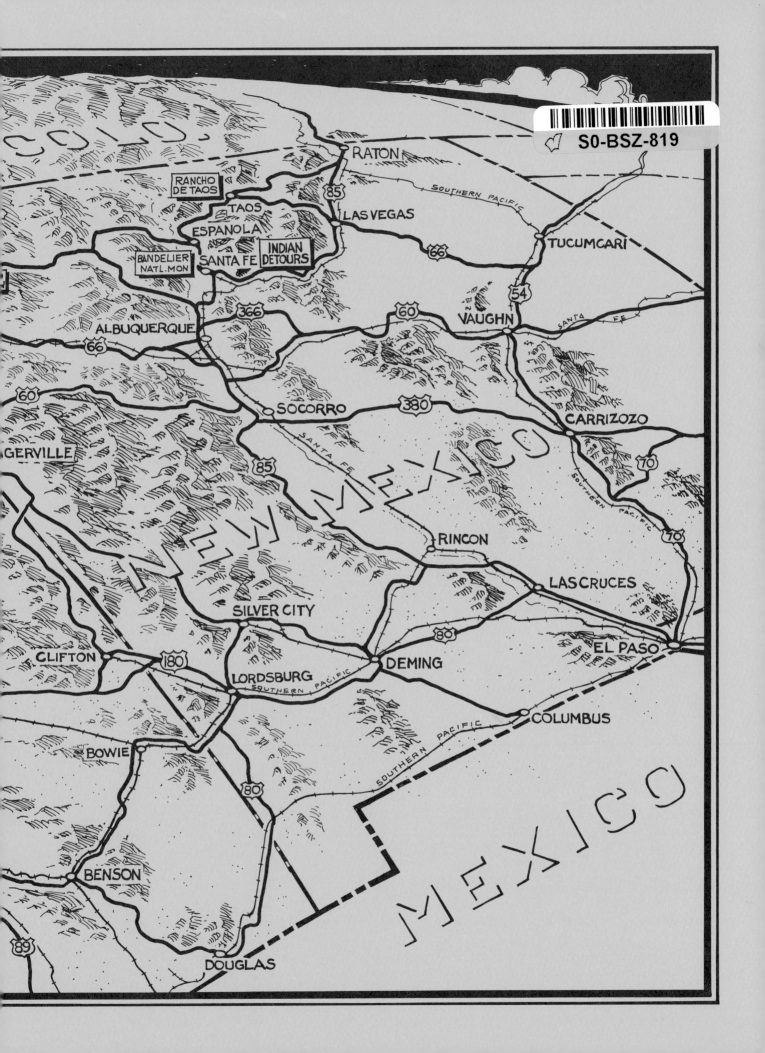

P. James Hahn

2425 W. 16 St.

Wilmington Del. 19806

May. 16, 1989

Trails Begin Where Rails End

*Early-day Motoring Adventures
in the West and Southwest*

Albert D. Manchester

Trans-Anglo Books • Glendale California

Cover and Frontispiece Paintings by John Signor

Back Cover Photo

A family on an automobile outing, circa 1925, has stopped at the portal of one of several tunnels on the Corley Mountain Highway in Colorado. Built on the roadbed of the Colorado Springs-Cripple Creek District Railroad, the highway was operated as a toll road from 1924 to 1939, when it became a free public highway known as the Gold Camp Road. **Pikes Peak Library District**

Table of Contents Photo

Two Packard Eights of the Indian Detours pause in La Manga Pass, Colorado, elevation 10,200 feet. It is late spring or early summer, circa 1927; snow is still in evidence in protected areas, such as the one at upper left. This looks like one of the photos that would appear in ads for the Santa Fe Railway's Indian Detours, in the National Geographic. *Santa Fe Railway photographer Edward Kemp went along on this trip, which may have been a run just to get some publicity shots.*
Edward Kemp, Museum of New Mexico Collection

TRAILS BEGIN WHERE RAILS END

Library of Congress Cataloging-in-Publication Data

Manchester, Albert D.
    Trails begin where rails end.

    Bibliography: p.
    Includes index.
    1. Automobiles—Southwest, New — Touring — History.   2. Automobiles — West (U.S.) — Touring — History.   3. Southwest, New — Description and travel. 4. West (U.S.) — Description and travel.   I. Title.
GV1024.M32   1987   917.8   87-10897
ISBN 0-87046-081-1

Published by TRANS-ANGLO BOOKS a division of INTERURBAN PRESS

P.O. Box 6444 • Glendale, California 91205

Printed and bound in the United States of America

For Chickey

The most beautiful adventures are not those we go to seek.
Robert Louis Stevenson

Acknowledgements

Although the writing of a book such as this may not take a very long time, the gathering of the material will have been going on for almost a lifetime of personal experience and study. Unfortunately, I can't thank all of the people who helped me over the years. Many of them have passed out of mind, too many of them out of this life.

Some of the material in this book appeared in other forms in automobile and motorcycle magazines, but especially in *Car Collector and Car Classics,* edited by Donald R. Peterson. Other people who helped in recent years were Mary M. Davis of Pikes Peak Library District, Colorado Springs; Robert Houchin, a dedicated collector of Indian Detours memorabilia; members of the Columbus, New Mexico Historical Society; and the library staffs at New Mexico State University, Las Cruces, New Mexico, the United States Air Force Academy, the Eisenhower Library, the Arizona Historical Society of Tucson, the History Library of the Museum of New Mexico, and the Thomas Branigan Memorial Library, Las Cruces, New Mexico.

Although they already know how I feel, I want to thank Arthur K. Hauser, my father-in-law, whose photographic expertise was, as always, invaluable and, again, I'll thank my wife, Chickey, who had many helpful suggestions along the way and who prepared the final manuscript.

ALBERT D. MANCHESTER
MAY 1987

Table of Contents

Somewhere in western New Mexico, circa 1930, a 1929 Cadillac belonging to the Indian Detours fleet has stopped to let a group of "dudes" alight. The Indian Detours allowed passengers on Santa Fe Railway trains a chance to stop off for a couple of days or more, and get off the beaten path for an intimate look at the majestic scenery, Indian pueblos, and ancient cliff dwellings in our great Southwest. All this, at a time when the train meant transportation and many Easterners thought New Mexico was a foreign country!

Margaret Wennips Moses Collection

Introduction

HEN I WAS VERY YOUNG my parents would always take me with them when they went to visit Aunt Louise and Uncle Andy. Louise and Andy had a goldfish pond in their backyard. The pond was probably not as large as it seems to me it must have been, but it was certainly large enough to fascinate a little boy who knew of no other such pond. Summer visits I would spend in the backyard, except when Aunt Louise would call me in for a bottle of soda pop. Since this was in Minnesota, I did not spend winter visits in the backyard. I can't remember what Louise and Andy did with those large goldfish in the wintertime.

During those winter visits, while my parents and Louise and Andy sat at the kitchen table and vied with each other to come up with the most boring conversations they could think of (or so it seemed to me), I would retire to the dining room. There was a closet off the dining room that was stacked with old *National Geographic Magazines*, a collection dating back more or less to the days of Hammurabi, as I recall. I'm sure that if you looked in the darkest corner of the closet, you could have found a few early issues carved in stone. I would curl up in a big soft rocking chair that was covered with black horsehide and read the *Geographics*, one after another, rocking slowly back and forth next to the clanking radiator as I did so.

Oh, I didn't actually read the magazines. I've never met anybody who's ever read an entire *National Geographic* from cover to cover. What I liked to do was look at the advertisements and the photographs and read the photo captions. You could always learn almost everything you had to know about the article from the photo captions. And the cranky black and white photography was wonderful. You could study photos of naked cannibals and the gates of Chinese cities where the heads of bandits were stuck up on stakes as a warning to other bandits. Peasants with bad teeth and dressed in outrageous costumes posed on mountain paths in European countries that no longer exist. Places like Montenegro. Most of the world looked as though it had not been discovered by anybody until the *Geographic* writer or photographer stumbled into it.

I liked some *Geographic* stories a lot better than others. I have to admit that I was not taken with articles that were called things like, "Toothy Denizens of the Deep," "Baltimore's Lovely Bird Friends," or "My Life Among Arizona Spiders." Often illustrated in terrible color. No, the stories I liked best were those that told of treks across forbidden lands or sailing expeditions to impossible corners of the globe. Trips into places where a machine gun, such as the light, pan-fed Lewis, might come in handy. A trip where everybody packed a gun because you couldn't trust the "natives," who truly looked like natives are supposed to look. Stories like that were more like those movies in which everybody wore a pith helmet.

As I progressed into the late 1920s, *Geographically*

A Santa Fe Railway "Harveycoach" was stopped along the road in this view, circa 1930. The location is thought to be near Glorieta Pass in New Mexico; note the Santa Fe Railway bridge in the background, advertising "THE GRAND CANYON LINE" to passersby on the Indian Detours trail. **Dorothy Raper Miller Collection**

speaking, I came across advertisements for something called the Indian Detours. The ads usually carried a photograph of a touring car loaded with well dressed folks, the car heading up a dirt road, and way off in the distance you could see mountains. It looked like good country, a clean place to be. It was, I read, our own Southwest, where, if you took a tour with the Indian Detours, you could visit mountains and mesas, modern Indian pueblos, ruins of ancient pueblos, cliff dwellings, romantic towns settled by the conquistadores . . . well, just all manner of romantic things. It looked like it would be a really swell trip; every time I saw an Indian Detours ad I wished I could have gone with them. I had a feeling that I'd missed something that would have been important to me.

By the time I moved to New Mexico, many years later and after adventures of my own in other parts of the world, the Indian Detours had long since ceased to exist. Along in the 1970s I came to know an older man by the name of Norbert Staab who one day told me about a burglary he had suffered. Among the things taken, he said, were priceless, irreplaceable artifacts of the Indian Detours, many of them of silver. He had once been a driver for the Indian Detours, he explained, but that was a long time ago. Before you were born, he said, laughing, apparently thinking how ridiculous it would be to imagine I had heard of the Indian Detours.

Of course, I knew at once what he was talking about. I spent many pleasant hours with Norbert after that, chatting with him about the Detours. He introduced me to several other ex-employees of the Indian Detours, drivers and couriers, all whom I met now gone. Lucille Stacy was especially helpful, once we got past her shy-

ness. I still wonder that she was able to be a courier, meeting new people every day.

The early 1930s, when this book ends, doesn't seem to me a long time ago. I've spent so much time studying the early days of motoring that sometimes I forget that not everybody has heard of automobiles called the Winton, the Matheson, the Hupmobile. Most folks seem too consider a relatively recent Studebaker to be a quaint machine, while I'm thinking about automobiles that ceased to be manufactured a lifetime ago.

The Great Depression is, I feel, a great separating point in our national life. Many automobile marques became history in the 1930s. Ways of thinking and feeling about life changed so dramatically during that decade that folks from the 1920s meeting people in the 1940s could be strangers to each other. The 1930s was a Big Burnout. In any event, we keep passing through an Ellis Island of change in this country, one generation a stranger to the next.

I discovered this fairly recently, mainly, I suppose, because I've now arrived at an age where I don't mind sitting back and listening to older people talk. One of my friends, Harold Collyer, died a few years ago. I used to visit him often, although not as often as I now wished I had. His eyesight was poor and he could just barely walk. He was almost ninety. He was forced to drink his Scotch mixed with milk, and he was not allowed to smoke more than a pack of cigarettes a day, so he smoked the strongest he could buy. Harold had more verve, he had more adventure and romance in his soul, than almost anybody I knew, except possibly his wife, Kay, who was almost as old. They seemed not afraid of the future. Life was all rather exciting to them, whatever it was that happened to be going on.

One of Harold's great interests was the early days of motoring, of which he had been an enthusiastic participant. We traded stories and literature on the subject. One of Harold's adventures is included here, as well as a couple of my own. My only excuse for daring to include my own adventures in a book about the early days of motoring is the fact that the trips took place in western and northern Canada, and in Alaska, over thirty years ago when that area was still something of a frontier. Thirty years ago seems to me to qualify as history.

The title of the book, TRAILS BEGIN WHERE RAILS END, is taken from the only magazine article Harold Collyer ever had published. The story was in a nature magazine back in the 1920s and was about a motor trip he and Kay took to Colorado. When I knew them, they couldn't even find a copy of the story. Harold was one of the most frustrated would-be writers I've ever met, his literary sensibilities much finer than my own. I don't think he'll mind if I borrow his title for a book about some aspects of a subject we both enjoyed discussing so much, the early days of motoring in the West and Southwest.

Opposite, alongside ads for Miami Beach, Florida, and the Tucson Sunshine-Climate Club, one could find ads for the Indian Detours in National Geographic Magazine, *circa 1927.* **John Signor Collection**

Breaking Trail

ALASKA. SEPTEMBER, 1953.

I turned east off the road to Eagle and headed for Dawson City, Yukon Territory, riding away from the Fortymile River on my old Harley-Davidson, up onto the ridges I would follow into the Yukon. The trees thinned, became increasingly more stunted and scattered, and then nonexistent as I climbed above timberline, which is quite low when you get that far north. The "road" deteriorated until it became just two wheel ruts along the top of the mountain ridges, a roller coaster trail, mud-slippery but exhilerating.

It was easy for me to enjoy the solitude and the remoteness because I knew—I *knew*—the old long-stroker chugging beneath me was not going to seize up or fall apart. My Harley was an ex-Army bike, a 45 cid side-valver that was geared down for military work and powered by a low compression R-type engine. A couple of the fins had been busted off the front aluminum head. This was a motorcycle with a story, a veteran of the war,

The Narrows on the Crystal Park Auto Road in Colorado, altitude 7,060 feet. The grade of the road ranged from two to eight percent and the road climbed to a maximum altitude of 7,945 feet above sea level. A fleet of specially built, mountain-climbing Packards like the one pictured here was owned and operated by the road company. The 30-mile toll road is shown here circa 1910.

Pikes Peak Library District

a machine with a fifty mission crush. But that wasn't why I had bought it. I bought the bike because it was the only motorcycle for sale in Anchorage, Alaska, the spring of 1953. It had cost me $175.00.

That was back when o.d. meant olive drab, which was the color of the 1941 Harley when I bought it. Two weeks later you wouldn't have recognized the GI bike: grease and dirt cleaned away, tuned up, chopped fenders, painted a jaunty red and black. It looked like a speedy little hunk of iron. It wasn't. Top speed was only about 55 mph, which was, however, quite fast enough when you keep in mind the rocky, sandy, muddy roads that connected Alaska's scattered settlements.

The 45 side-valver was the "smallest of the big twins," introduced in 1929 to compete with 45 cid models then being made by Excelsior and Indian, although it was never as popular as either of them. The Harley 45 was just not very spritely, even in civvies, and it certainly wasn't very popular with the muscle riders of the day, most of whom rode heavyweights. But the GI bike was just right for the Last Frontier as we knew it then. It was light enough to manhandle through the truly rough places, and it carried a skid plate to protect the engine, transmission and chain. The engine fins were extra long to help dissipate heat during long periods of low-gear slogging. Quite by chance, I had bought what may well have been the only motorcycle in Alaska that was built for boondocking. By September of 1953 I had explored all of Alaska I could reach on my motorcycle, and so I set off on a ride into Canada's Yukon Territory,

Riding the ridges into the Yukon Territory, I was far above the timberline. The Yukon River lies in fog beyond the farthest hill. This is as good as the road got; I had to ford small streams.
Albert Manchester

into the Klondike . . .

A thin, arctic sun was out as I rode the muddy trail toward the Yukon Territory. The valley of the Yukon River, a few miles to the north, was filled with fog. Far below me the creek beds were lined with shimmering yellow aspen leaves. (In New Mexico where I live now, the aspens exist only in the highest elevations.) Beyond

My old GI Harley down on Alaska's Kenai Peninsula in June of 1953. By this time I had the old bike all cleaned up and repainted. The old military motorcycle was a good boondocker.
Albert Manchester

the creek beds, beyond the Yukon, right over to the other side of the world, lay pure wilderness. I was riding along what was at the time the very last trail into that part of the North.

An old roadhouse, possibly dating from the days of the Gold Rush, used to sit just west of the Alaska-Yukon border, low log structures along the south side of the trail, a small log building about the size of a one-car garage—the "bar"—on the north side of the trail. Four Indian boys about my age (I was nineteen) tumbled out of the roadhouse as I bounced into the yard and cut the engine.

They were from villages on the Yukon. Their eyes popped open with wonder as they marveled at that wonderful example of the white man's culture, my hot, mud-filthy Army 45. It was the first real live motorcycle any of them had ever seen.

Determined to thrill my territorial cousins right down to their longjohns, I introduced them to the motorcycle: spark control (left) and throttle (right) on the handlebars, shifting lever (three speeds) on the left side of the tank. Clutch pedal (left) and brake pedal (right) on the footrests. Instrument panel on the fuel and oil tanks. To culminate my act, I showed them how to kick-start the engine. The boys winced satisfactorily and then laughed at the racket as I opened the throttle wide. (No muffler.) Animals for miles around must have raised their heads in surprise and fear, as in *Bambi*. They had heard it for the first time . . . *the call of the wild biker.*

That night an old miner I met in the bar told me to be careful. Winter was close, he said. A few other miners, placer miners from the creek bottoms below the mountain, spilled out their pent-up conversation on each other. The small room reeked of booze, tobacco smoke, kerosene fumes. The "bartender" lay on a couch behind the short bar, his mouth open, one arm dangling to the floor. The few customers made their own drinks, put their own money into the ancient cash register, and took their change. When I suggested that the bartender looked like he was dead, the men laughed and said he was just his own best customer.

The night was cold when I went back outside to cross the road to the dark bunkhouse. Thin ice had formed over the puddles in the road. The aurora borealis hovered over the roadhouse and the mountain, great bands of weaving, flickering light that stretched from the north all the way into the south. The light fell out of the sky like unrolling curtains trying to reach down to us on the mountain. Was the aurora the opening act of the coming winter? Kids used to believe what older people told them, or at least they worried sufficiently over it to make themselves uncomfortable.

The next morning I rode into the Yukon Territory and dropped down to the Yukon River. Yellowing aspens lined both sides of the road and formed a roof over my head, and the trail was slippery with wet, yellow leaves. Sunlight filtered through the trees to form a beautiful tunnel. The air was musty with the smell of decaying leaves. The ride was like being in a time-tunnel into another world, which was exactly how it turned out.

Dawson City, the heart of the Klondike, had harbored 30,000 to 40,000 "stampeders" during the Gold Rush at the turn of the century. About 500 people remained in Dawson in 1953, including some of the original participants of the Gold Rush. The old men would tell you about the Gold Rush if you dared to ask them. They sat in chairs on Front Street, soaking up the sun. A few of them suggested I get my skinny Yank tail and my cockeyed machine back into Alaska . . . unless I had made plans for wintering over in Dawson.

Dawson was a sprawling Gay Nineties junkyard. I poked around in abandoned houses and cabins, some still partly furnished. Calendars from decades before hung askew on water-stained walls. Doors creaked in the wind. I explored derelict sternwheelers on the beach and I climbed over rusting mining machinery in empty lots. I rode my Harley up along the creeks into the abandoned gold fields where I rummaged through rotting cabins. Using a rusty pie plate from one of the cabins, I panned for gold. Plenty of "color" was still showing up in the Klondike gravel. I still have a small volume I found on a shelf in a cabin, *The Poetical Works of John Keats*. Who was it that whiled away winter days in that remote place, penciling off favorite passages?

He mourns that day so soon has glided by:
E'en like the passage of an angel's tear
That falls through the clear ether silently.*

Whoever he was, he even took it upon himself to make a few "corrections," changing a word here and there. Presumptuous fellow! I sat on a creek bank to read a few poems myself, then pocketed the book.

Alex, one of the old men who had arrived when Dawson was a wild and woolly town, had keys to all the old saloons and dance halls. He took me on a tour one day, filling my head with tales of the famous and flamboyant and the lonely stampeders who once crowded those places. He had known many of them, he said. And he wanted to get one thing straight, once and for all: Dawson was not as dangerous a place as the fictionalized accounts of those days would have a person think. Most of the stampeders were gentlemen, men who would never think of plucking a man's poke even though his celebrating had overwhelmed him. A drunk could expect to wake up with his stake still in his pocket. Anyway, at least one steely-eyed Mountie was always on hand in Dawson to make sure the boys behaved.

---

*Keats, John. *The Poetical Works of John Keats*, MacMillan and Co., New York, 1894. Page 40.

Perched on the road above Bear Creek Canyon, Yukon Territory, another view of my 1941 Harley-Davidson "45," the smallest of the big twins. My ride into Dawson City in the fall of 1953 was a ride through time as well as space. **Albert Manchester**

Alex had been an entertainer in the old days. Dressed in a style from the last century, he did a soft-shoe routine for me on the stage in one place, raising a little dust. He must have heard some music of his own, a distant ragtime echo.

One of the old saloons was still operating. The customers were few but dedicated, one of them a blond fellow of about thirty who announced enthusiastically that he was dying of tuberculosis. He liked to recite the poems of Robert Service, the Klondike poet, and he did so with skill and emotion. Alex and I sipped our beers and listened. Then the man decided to sing "Squaws Along the Yukon," a dismal ditty of the times, one of the lines of which runs, "and squaws are good enough for me." A handsome, blind Indian woman had been sitting with a white man at a table on one side of the room. She rose to her feet, followed the blond man's voice across the room, snatched him out of his chair, and knocked him flat on the floor.

"Squaws are good enough for any white man," she told the respectful gathering.

We all cheered.

The next day even I could see it was time to go; snow lay just outside of town on top of the mountains. Gray clouds skudded over. The air was cold. I shouldn't have spent so much time in Dawson. I fueled up with gas that cost 85¢ per Imperial gallon, gasoline that had arrived in Dawson City in fifty-five gallon drums hauled down from Whitehorse on river boats, and then I roared back under the aspens and climbed back into the mountains . . . and right into the first snowstorm of the season. Snow built up on the muddy windshield. The trail was wet, slippery, then became white. I had trouble keeping to the trail. The valley below was hidden by swirling snow. I chugged past the roadhouse—I didn't dare stop—and at last skidded down the other side of the mountains, out of the snow, to the Fortymile River. Relieved to have survived the ride, I kicked the Harley up to a good speed as I thundered around the curves, trailing a mist of dust that drifted off the road and down to the river far below me . . .

So that's the way it was, over thirty years ago, motorcyling on our last frontier. It was a good place to be and a good time to be there. The moose, bear, and sourdoughs didn't notice that my bike was an example of 1920s engineering, a mechanical contemporary of the Model A, inexpensive, reliable, "forgiving," a motorcycle a kid would dare ride into the Klondike. A classic American machine, the GI Harley was designed with rugged, flatheaded simplicity, a motorcycle from an era when most folks expected to do for themselves.

There were no motorcycle agencies, no motorcycle

The old Harley "45" was a motorcycle a kid could trust, even if he took a wild notion to head into the Klondike.   **Albert Manchester**

repair shops in Alaska. We bought engine oil at air strips and we mailed to California for any parts we needed. But my veteran never left me stranded, and any repairs I had to make in the hinterland were accomplished with the simple tools I was able to carry with me. You didn't mind being out on the last trail at the end of civilization if you had some reasonable hope of getting back, or getting on to where you wanted to go.

Americans began driving into the wilderness beyond the railheads as soon as they had machines that would start in that direction. I said *start*. No doubt many of those early automobiles are still out there in the deserts and mountains. Part of the scenery, sinking slowly into the earth.

Many of us are fascinated by motoring stories about excursions into sparsely settled or undeveloped areas. It's the almost irresistible, romantic lure of distant mountains, forests, plains. We want to be on our own in that far scenery, in or on a machine of our own, going or stopping when it so pleases us. Exploring. It's in the genes.

* * *

IN 1903 A TRAVELER could get from San Francisco to New York in four or five days by train for a cost of about twenty bucks. Why, then, would a man risk a $3000 automobile, to say nothing of life or limb, trying to drive said automobile from San Francisco to New York? For one thing, for a fifty-dollar bet.

Dr. Horatio N. Jackson, a thirty-one-year-old Vermonter, had wintered over in California after a few

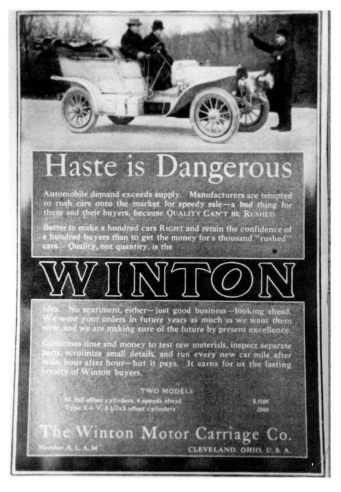

years in the Klondike. He must have made a bit of money in the Yukon, enough to buy a Locomobile (a steamer) and enough to dine at the University Club. Legend has it that Jackson overheard another gentleman at the club state he was willing to bet $50 that no automobile could cross the United States, even if the driver had ninety days to make the trip. Dr. Jackson, a completely converted "automobilist," is said to have jumped up to cover the bet.

Not so fast, cautioned Sewell Crocker, the chauffeur Jackson hired to accompany him. The Locomobile, he said, might not be the machine for the trip. And just why the hell not? Jackson asked. After all, a Locomobile steamer had been the first automobile to conquer Pikes Peak, back in '01. The Locomobile was made from Stanley Steamer patents. It was a fine machine. Maybe so, Crocker continued, but a steamer needs plenty of care, to say nothing of water. And they were going to be crossing some mighty parched country. They wouldn't be able to carry enough water. Jackson hadn't thought about that. What could they do? Buy a gas car, if you really have to go, Crocker said.

Jackson settled on a 1903 Winton, which was either new or just slightly used. Sources vary on this, just as they vary on the spelling of Crocker's name. The Winton was, however, apparently as good as new. It cost $3,000. Possibly Jackson traded the Locomobile in on it. In any event, the Winton was probably as good a choice as he could have made at the time. It was, along about then, one of our better cars, manufactured in Cleveland, Ohio, by Alexander Winton, an immigrant Scots engineer who had been building automobiles since 1897. Although known today only to the most devoted of automobile buffs, the Wintons were well known in their day and were manufactured until 1924. Race cars built by Winton set many records in the very early years, a few of the cars in the hands of the burly, legendary Barney Oldfield.

Dr. Jackson's transcontinental boondocker was no race car; it was, except for the installation of a twenty gallon gasoline tank, a stock model. The two-cylinder, twenty h.p. engine was cranked on the side. It was chain-driven, steered on the right, and had no windshield. This was a gas-buggy, high wheels and high center of gravity. Except for the smell of the contraption, the old family nag would have had a hard time distinguishing it from any other buggy on the streets.

All of the other twenty or thirty cross-country automobile attempts had so far foundered, and most of them had failed in the Southwest. Jackson and Crocker decided to head north toward Oregon where they would connect with the Oregon Trail and then work their way into the Midwest. They pulled away from Market Street at 1:00 p.m. on the 23rd of May, their car loaded with tools (including the *sine qua non* of early motoring, shovel and axe), spare parts, block and tackle, firearms, a camping outfit, and gasoline and water. Some of the darker parts of the North American map awaited them.

Not that the area west of the Pecos—most of it, at any rate—was still a raging wilderness in 1903. In 1860, for example, traffic down the Santa Fe Trail amounted to 9,000 travelers, 3,000 wagons, almost 28,000 oxen, and 6,000 mules. (Apparently nobody counted the horses.) Railroads had broken across Arizona and New Mexico in the 1880s. The Union Pacific had tracks across the country up where Jackson and Crocker planned to cross. Many thousands of miles of roads did exist in the United States, although all the better roads were on either coast or in the Midwest, anywhere where enough people lived to pay the taxes that built the roads. Farm country tended to have better roads than places like the great deserts or the Rocky Mountain country, although trails did exist there, from ranch to ranch, ranch to town, mine to town. But even roads in the more populated parts of the country were generally no better than the country lanes that had existed back in Civil War or Revolutionary War times. On the other hand, the railroad system in 1903 was not vastly different than it is now, although probably more extensive and much more indispensable.

In many places the road system was worse than it had been before the expansion of the railroads. With the railroads came speed and the comfort away from days and days of plodding along behind animals in mud or dust. Many old roads deteriorated. What roads did exist were matters of local concern, and road building and maintenance would cease at any point where local interest and money ceased. People who did not travel by train did not get farther than a day's ride away from home, twenty or thirty miles in a horse and buggy. Everybody knew the country where they happened to live; no signs were posted for the benefit of cross-country travelers, because by 1903 nobody traveled across the country except by train. Bicycle enthusiasts (many, many) had lobbied for better roads, and some had been built, but mainly in the eastern states. Bicyclists were not yet challenging the continent, although in 1897 twenty men of the 25th Bicycle Corps, all black troops except for a white officer, had pedaled 1,900 miles from Fort Missoula, Montana, to St. Louis in 41 days, as far as is known the only long range bicycle tour ever made by the US Army. It was a grueling march that proved the far west was not ready for bicycles. Nor, after this experiment, was the Army ready for them.

Travel away from the railroads was full of surprises and disappointments, as Crocker and Jackson would soon find out. But one thing that modern readers discover from investigating these early trips is that many of the first cars were much better than we now give them credit for being. That old Harley 45 of mine was as rugged a machine as I've ever owned. Most of the old-timers had simplicity in their favor. In some early car advertising, manufacturers lauded the simplicity of their machines, as if this were a goal in itself. Not so crazy an idea. How many of us now dare to try to repair our own cars?

Get out and get under. Men who just a few years before had worked on nothing more complicated than a bicycle now probed the intimate parts of their automobiles. By today's standards, some astonishingly comprehensive repairs were attempted just along the roadside. Tires *were* a problem, more serious a problem than modern motorists realize; any moderately ambitious trip could result in some tire and tube work. Many cars left the garage with four or five spares on board.

Meanwhile, up in eastern Oregon, Jackson and Crocker wandered lost through the wilderness, forced to pour their good water into the Winton's radiator while they themselves drank foul water from alkaline puddles. They lost their cyclometers, their cooking gear. They ran out of gas. Crocker lost the coin toss and set off on foot for a town, Burns, which turned out to be almost thirty miles away. Good lad, he showed up in camp the next day on an old bicycle, loaded down with five gallons of fuel.

They ferried across the Snake River into Idaho and headed southeast with the Union Pacific track. The rains came. Stuck fast in mud, they would slosh ahead on foot, drive a stake into the ground, then pull the car forward with block and tackle. Nine times in one day, twenty-eight miles for the day. But they made Caldwell, Idaho, and the locals were so pleased that they threw a celebration for the determined motorists. At this time, at or near Caldwell, they picked up a passenger, a rugged-looking bull mutt they called Bud.

Passing through the Rocky Mountain states, the boys were in the absolute vanguard of the Motor Age in many towns. Cowboys, loggers, farmers, miners gathered around the chugging contraption to wonder at what man had wrought. Indians, seeing their first automobile, must have thrown up their hands in despair . . . a fire-belching machine that did not even have to stick to the iron trail!

Although still rare creatures in the West in 1903, automobiles had appeared here and there, a few locally made contraptions, but many good machines were being shipped in by rail. Colorado Springs, although hardly a typical western town, had about a dozen cars as early as 1900. By 1900 the automobile had become a plaything of the rich, to vie for their time with yachting, horses, and hunting. The wealthy denizens of the Rocky Mountain town brought in the snazziest machines they could buy, about an even mix of gasoline powered cars, steamers, and electrics. A *two*-car family owned a French Panhard, at the time one of the very best cars in the world. (The French were quite the pioneers of automobile manufacturing. The Panhard was noted for its craftsmanship and was the first production car to have pneumatic tires.) European cars, however, were not generally suited to our West. Their weight to engine capacity lagged behind the American cars, and for many years American cars were built with higher clearance. These differences were for a good reason. European roads were good; out of presumed military necessity, smooth roads such as the *routes nationals* of France had been common on the continent for many years.

Ten or twelve thousand automobiles were made in the United States in 1903, although Jackson, out there in Wyoming, certainly had no inkling of it. Out there, where he and Crocker went for thirty-six hours without seeing another human, he learned to let the Winton pull itself forward out of mud holes, a rope tied to a stake in front of the car winding itself up on the rear axle. They used this rope-around-the-axle trick sixteen times in one day. Terribly tough work, but, after all, Jackson had fifty bucks riding on the outcome of the expedition.

The Winton picked up wounds. When the ball bearings in a front wheel failed, Crocker was able to make repairs with the help of parts from a mowing machine and the lucky assistance of a coal mine mechanic. A broken connecting rod drove right through the crankcase near Rawlins, Wyoming. New parts were shipped in by rail from Ohio and the boys lost only five days.

(A layover for repairs in the 1950s on the Alaska Highway could take even longer while an order for parts rode south with a trucker, who bought the parts in Dawson Creek or Edmonton, and then shipped them north with another trucker. In 1952 I met a businessman and his family from Anchorage who had waited almost two weeks for parts for his new Chrysler, then had to do the repairs himself. This at a lonely outpost on the Highway without electricity or indoor plumbing. That was the only time I have ever seen an eight-holer outhouse. It would have been a miracle of coincidence if eight people had gathered there at the same time and for the same purpose. The owner of the business—gas station, restaurant, a few rude cabins—had killed a mother grizzly. Its cub was locked up in a storage building and would hide behind oil drums, running out in a mock attack to gum our hands when it didn't think we were looking. The Anchorage businessman, with plenty of time on his hands while he waited for his parts, helped me repair the hydraulic brakes of the '41 Chevrolet I was driving.)

New Goodrich tires were sent to Jackson from back east. When part of the steering mechanism was damaged, Crocker jury-rigged repairs with a length of pipe until they could locate a blacksmith. In the beginning of motoring, mechanical knowledge and blacksmithing were often part of the same skill.

With the Rockies behind them, it became apparent that Jackson, the "mad doctor," and his companions might just stand a chance of winning through. News of their passage started to be telegraphed ahead. Schools and work stopped in some towns as folks awaited the arrival of the transcontinental Winton, the first car many of them would see. The muddy gas-buggy rolled out of the west, an extra tire ringing its cyclopean headlamp, a tough white bulldog wearing driving goggles sitting between the two motorists. Quite a vision for some of those remote villages where little of interest happened except the passing weather and the passing trains.

News caught up with Jackson that two other cross-country automobile expeditions were chasing him. One of the cars was a curved-dash Oldsmobile, the other a Packard that had been specially geared for desert and mountain travel.

Jackson and Crocker hit the trail with new inspiration, driving from dawn to dark, sleeping where darkness caught them, spurning bath and bed of hotels, sleeping under the Winton in order to be on the road

Two Reos from about 1906 resting next to a tin-roofed adobe near Nogales. Such a touring car would have cost about $1,250. Note the five-gallon tins on the ground between the cars, and the spare tires draped over the hoods. **Arizona Historical Society Library/Tucson**

A Mountain of Evidence

The clean-cut greatness of REO performance looms up like a giant mountain.

Look at the endless string of real cups and trophies won by REO cars at every kind of work that a motor-car can do:—in climbing contests from the New Hampshire peaks to the California Coast Range; endurance tests against the worst roads and weather that the United States can furnish; and speed, efficiency and economy trials convincing beyond parallel.

Look at the many cars of immensely higher rating and pretension from which these trophies were wrested.

Above all, look at how these REO performances are duplicated in daily use in owners' hands for half the price and half the operating-cost that other motor-cars demand.

If your eyes are open to what is going on you cannot help seeing this mountain of record facts. And if you want the most and best motoring for your money, how can you help sending for the REO catalogue which shows why these things are so?

REO 16-20 horse-power, 94-inch wheel-base. Detachable tonneau. Two speeds and reverse. REO disc clutch, 40 miles an hour. Full lamp equipment. **$1,250**

2-passenger Runabout $650   4-passenger Runabout $675

All prices f. o. b. Lansing

R. M. OWEN & CO., Lansing, Mich.
General Sales Agents

The Reo automobile was the brainchild of Ransom E. Olds, who was also the father of the Oldsmobile. This ad is from a 1906 Munsey Magazine; *according to the specs, one could attain a speed of 40 mph in this machine, which seems fast enough.* **Albert Manchester**

each day with the sun. They rolled into Omaha on the 12th of July, Chicago the 17th. Heroes now, crowds turned out to see them as they pounded across Indiana in the clattering Winton. In Ohio, Alexander Winton offered to give the car a factory overhaul. The offer was refused by Jackson, who didn't want his private expedition suddenly turned into a Winton promotional stunt. The Packard and the Oldsmobile, still coming behind him, were factory cars being driven by professional teams. Jackson was the only amateur in the running.

And he won, the first man to drive a car all the way across the United States under its own power, except for those mud holes where a team of horses had become necessary to rescue them. The Winton Motor Carriage Company posted $25,000, stating the money would go to whomever could prove that Jackson hadn't made the trip himself. The money was never claimed. The Smithsonian Institution investigated the expedition and said, yes, the boys had won through from coast-to-coast fair and square. The Winton, with some of its original equipment, now rests in the Smithsonian.

Jackson, Crocker and Bud rolled up to the Holland House at 5th Avenue and 30th Street, New York City, at 4:30 a.m., July 26th, 1903, *sixty-four days* down the trail from San Francisco. They had driven the Winton at least 4,500 miles. The Packard was still struggling across Nebraska, the Oldsmobile out of touch someplace in Wyoming.

So Jackson had won his $50 bet. The trip, including the purchase of the Winton, had cost him about $8,000. He was twenty pounds lighter than when he left San Francisco. Was it all worth it? You bet, even though his cross-country record lasted less than a month. He was the first; pretty hard to beat that.

Returning to his home in Vermont, the conquering hero was arrested in Burlington, Vermont, for exceeding the six mile-per-hour speed limit. That cost Jackson another $12.99. He lived a long and useful lfe, although he never again took to the wilderness roads. He served in World War I, later becoming one of the founders of the American Legion. He was a newspaper publisher, owner of a radio station, and a bank president. Back in '03 he showed everybody he could be a very determined man.

* * *

In August of 1903, less than a month after Dr. Jackson arrived in New York, his record fell to a Packard Model F driven by Tom Fetch and Marius Krarup, who drove about 3,500 miles from San Francisco to New York in sixty-one days.

Interesting that it should be a Packard to beat the Winton's time.

James Ward Packard's *first* automobile, before he started making his own, was a Winton. Packard bought the twelfth machine Winton made, in 1898. The new car broke down several times during the trip to Packard's house, finally pulling into the yard behind a team of horses, an ignominious arrival for a proud man. He tried to return the car to Winton, get his $1,000 refunded (a thousand bucks would buy a lot of steak dinners in 1898). Winton would have none of it. When Packard suggested that neither Winton's car nor his business practice could stand close inspection, Alexander Winton told the irate customer that he should build his own car if he thought he could do any better.

As it turned out, Winton threw down his gauntlet in front of the wrong man. Packard was an engineer. His family had money. Just fifteen months later Packard's first car, the Model A, rolled out of the shop. Packards were built for forty years after the last Winton was built, and right from the start they were rock-solid reliable automobiles, conservative but well made, one of the best marques ever manufactured in the United States.

1903 was a Packard year, the year of the Model F. The Model F won the New York-Rochester five hundred mile run, the Automobile Club of America's nonstop one hundred mile endurance run, the Chicago nonstop one hundred miler, and the five hundred mile New York-to-Boston race. The record cross-country run just frosted the cake.

What kind of car was this indomitable Model F of 1903? It weighed 2,300 pounds and cost $2,500. Its single-cylinder engine produced 12 h.p. at 850 rpm, and with a good tail wind it could achieve 40 mph. As with many American cars of the era, the engine was mounted under the middle of the car. A foot brake acted on the rear wheels, a hand brake on the transmission. The chain-driven car also featured a removable tonneau (rear seats) and an automatic spark advance that was a Packard innovation. This little car startled the people in Colorado Springs when Fetch and Krarup chugged through town in July. Imagine, the Springs folks said to each other, all the way across from San Francisco,

through Reno and Salt Lake City and even over the Tennessee Pass. Maybe, just maybe the danged contraptions were not a plaything after all.

The curved-dash Oldsmobile appeared out of the hinterland in September. The curved-dash Olds, by the way, is the car that inspired the song, "In My Merry Oldsmobile." Over 15,000 of them were built.

Coast-to-coast in one year, three automobiles. The car was showing some muscle, "automobilism" was gaining ground in more ways than one. The development of metals, rubber and other essential materials could just keep pace with the rapidly growing industry.

The first decade of the century was a period of intense automotive experimentation. Engines were stuck in behind, in the middle, in front. Propulsion could be by electricity, steam, gasoline, compressed air, different kinds of exotic gases. Gasoline vehicles became more popular than electrics because they were more powerful than the electrics and had a wider range. Even by 1910 an electric would go only about eighty miles on a single

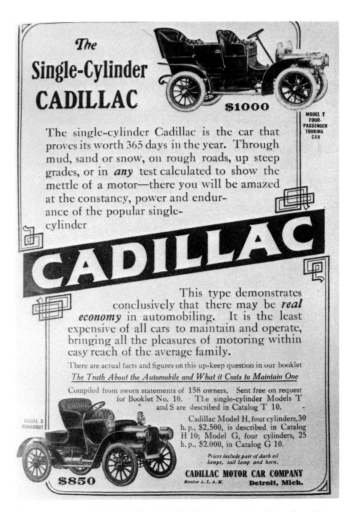

Two versions of the Cadillac Model T. As noted in the advertising copy, one could buy a four-cylinder model for $2,500. In 1908, Cadillac won the prestigious Dewar Trophy. Three Cadillacs were completely disassembled, their parts mixed, and then reassembled. They were then driven on a 500-mile endurance run at Brooklands track, and finished with a perfect score. **Albert Manchester Collection**

The Davis auto party in 1908 or 1909 in Tucson, Arizona, as they prepare to launch themselves into the wilderness for a trip to San Xavier Mission, about 10 miles south of town.
Arizona Historical Society Library/Tucson

charge. The electric was considered a town car, a car a gentleman could buy for his wife, a car for the gentleman who didn't venture out onto America's rough country roads, the car for the man who was appalled by the noisy, smelly, complicated gas-buggies. A few men preferred steamers, and there was nothing impotent about them.

Since we have had few steamers built in the past half century, the machine is now almost unknown. In its day there were *many* people who preferred it. It was quiet, simple, and smoother even than the smoothest gasoline powered automobile on the road today. There were, however, fears about the boilers, but these fears were mostly unfounded. The early steamers were slow to build up enough steam for a trip; but the last steamers built, the Dobles, could build up a head of steam in 90 seconds and get 1,500 miles on 24 gallons of water.

We have noted that a Locomobile steamer conquered Pikes Peak in 1901. The first gasoline car to climb to the top of the mountain, a Buick, did not arrive until 1913. Stanley Steamers were used in Colorado where roads were too steep for the early gas-buggies. In 1906, a Stanley Steamer called the Beetle broke the mile and the kilometer records at Ormond Beach, Florida, while traveling at 127 mph and 121 mph. In 1907, another Stanley Steamer, the Rocket, was whipping along the beach at an estimated 197 mph when it became *airborne*, flew for about a hundred feet, and was destroyed. The Stanley brothers so regretted the injuries the driver suffered that they gave up racing their cars. It wasn't until 1927 that a gasoline car officially exceeded the Rocket's speed on the beach. Whatever faults the steamers may have had, they certainly were not sluggish.

The early gasoline engines came in many more versions than today. Air-cooled, water-cooled, two-stroke,

four-stroke, valveless, single cylinder to six cylinder. They were set up horizontally, vertically, or in a vee; installed transversely or in line with the frame. Ignition could be hot tube (very early), magneto, coil and battery, or magneto and coil and battery. Final drive could be in front or rear, by chain, belt, or shaft. Steering was by wheel or tiller. Engineers experimented. The car evolved quickly through the decade until some of them, such as the 1905 Mercedes, were already astonishingly like the cars we drive today, although certainly not as standardized. A driver moving from car to car could be faced with a bewildering number of gear changes and gear changing patterns. As the cars grew speedier through the decade, their center of gravity descended toward the roadway. Even American machines came to look less and less like motorized buckboards.

* * *

ANOTHER HORSELESS CARRIAGE that conquered North America was the Franklin Model A that Lester Whitman and Clayton Carris drove from San Francisco to New York in 1904. Their record run was only thirty-two days, almost halving the cross-country driving time in only one year. Their route was fairly direct, through Ogden and Laramie, a jog down to Denver, then through Omaha, Chicago, Cleveland, Albany, and so to New York City.

Lester Whitman was a forty-three-year-old mechanic and driver who had settled in California from his native New England. Clayton Carris was only twenty-seven, but he was sufficiently well known as a driver by the Franklin Company of Syracuse, New York, for them to hire him to accompany Whitman in the attempt to break the record. It should be pointed out that endurance runs and races were wonderful advertising for the

The elegant Davis party at San Xavier Mission, proof positive that they made it all the way. A good pair of photos of an early automobile outing. **Arizona Historical Society Library/Tucson**

cars that survived such tests, so most of the manufacturers submitted models to such punishment at one time or another.

The car the boys drove was a light runabout that weighed only 1,050 pounds, which gave it an advantage in sand and mud. It's much easier to pull a light car out of a mud hole than a heavy one. Except for an extra-large gasoline tank, the Franklin was a chain-driven stock model with a 10 h.p. four-cylinder, cross-mounted engine. The machine was priced at $1,500, $200 more if you wanted the optional tonneau.

The Franklin engine was air-cooled, and the marque developed into possibly our finest air-cooled automobile before the company succumbed in 1934. Reportedly it continued to build aviation engines after that date, but the Franklin automobile became history. It had been the choice of many wealthy people. A custom-built Franklin could cost $9,000 to $10,000. It did have its problems, however. Air-cooled engines always require a heavier grade of oil than used in water-cooled engines, so the Franklin could be a devil of a hard starter during cold weather. And if the engine overheated, it could be hard to stop, the gasoline vapors "dieseling" until the frustrated driver jammed the car into gear and let out the clutch.

Whitman and Carris had their own problems with the Franklin engine overheating. With the prevailing wind on their stern, and having to drive slowly because of atrocious roads, or no roads at all in bad weather, their engine was often on the verge of seizing. But it never did, and although they averaged 150 miles per day, they had one day's run of 325 miles. Not so bad.

* * *

GASOLINE. How did those early motorists out in the vast heartland of America ever find enough fuel? They did, of course. In hardware stores, general merchandise stores, even grocery stores. The gasoline arrived by train or wagon in remote towns, and it was used for local automobiles and motorcycles, boats, and stationary engines such as pump engines or engines used in different kinds of mills. The gasoline was out there, not in large quantities, and it was sold from large drums or in five gallon tin cans. A traveler carried all he dared pack on board, and it was a much inferior product compared to what is used today. Two gallons of modern gasoline has the oomph of three or four gallons of the old stuff. The five gallon gasoline tins became ubiquitous material for patching roofs and sheds. They were cut open and just nailed on. If the gasoline had to be first pumped out of a drum, it could be pumped into a five gallon milk can in order to get an accurate measure.

The gasoline of the day, derived from the production of kerosene, was often polluted with water and other foreign substances. A driver would carry a chamois skin and funnel. The chamois skin was placed in the funnel and the gasoline was filtered through it and into the tank. More often than not, a bit of water and rust or dirt would remain in the chamois after the gas had filtered through it. Gasoline was expensive, but of course the farther one happened to be from a railroad town, the more expensive it got. At one point, Dr. Jackson had to pay $1.05 per gallon.

With the gasoline in the tank, the operator now had to start his machine. It's interesting to pause and consider those first motorists, all of whom were born before the invention of what we now consider the first motor vehicles. None of those men had cut his teeth on the throttle of a gasoline engine, but as far as the Americans were concerned, it was love at first sight. We took to the automobile as if its assimilation into our society and culture had been predetermined by God. Just the natural order of things. Progress. There were very few detractors as we surrendered ourselves to the notion of going faster and farther while sitting down.

Granted that cars were different, and that many even of the same make had their own particular "combination," this is generally how it was done. Comes the hero, who had not seen a real live automobile until two weeks ago. Now he is an expert automobilist. Climb in, make sure brake is on, clutch pedal down, gear shift in neutral. Open valve between gasoline tank and carburetor. Open throttle slightly, push spark advance lever as far back as possible. "Tickle" carburetor, depressing the float a bit to allow some gasoline to flood in. Insert crank. Check to make sure ignition is *off*. Pull engine through a few times to get air-gasoline mixture into the cylinders. Turn on ignition. (Contact!) Grasp crank in four fingers, thumb along handle so that crank is not entirely grasped in the fist. (So that if the engine starts when you're not expecting it to, the handle won't be driven back into the hand, causing possible serious injury, even a broken arm.) Press down on crank. Coming up with the handle, the automobilist should feel compression. Pull through with enthusiasm. Engine should start. No? Try again. And again. Take off coat and roll up sleeves. Do not flood engine.

Small wonder that our hero, who has just been set adrift in the Industrial Age on his own, preferred to buy an electric for his wife if he could afford two cars. The electric starter was not used on gasoline cars until 1912, then not on all cars. Automobiles built through the 1930s could be cranked. Electrics remained a part of the driving scene well into the 1920s.

One woman who didn't need an electric was Alice Ramsey, who, with three companions, drove to California from New York in 1909. The first woman driver across the continent. Dusters, goggles, and veils into the setting sun. And just six years after Jackson's trip in the Winton. Their Maxwell was an open touring model with an American flag fluttering from a fender.

The Maxwell had been provided by the company for the promotional stunt to advertise the reliability of their cars. The Maxwell was a good car, one of our better mid-priced machines, and the fictional preference of Jack Benny, as listeners to the old radio show will recall. In order to find her way west of the Mississippi, Alice would often follow the telegraph poles that carried the most wires. As yet, the AAA Blue Books—guides for motorists—did not cover much of the territory out west. As one early traveler put it, "Until Chicago we were motorists, then we became pioneers."

Many of the early cross-country runs were promotional stunts, although relatively local touring became more common. Local auto clubs became popular and their outings would get the more timid motorists out into the country . . . at least to that point where the good roads ended. But in 1908 the Jacob M. Murdocks family, father, mother and kiddies, drove their machine from Pasadena to New York in thirty-two days.

Women drivers and families out in the vast hinterland of America. So even before 1910 it was possible to motor across the country and have reasonable expectations of arriving at the other side. It was still a lot more expensive and time consuming than riding the train, but it was also more adventurous. Being out there on their own in the great emptiness gave the early motorists a feeling that the country belonged to them, not the railroads, and that is probably what this ever-increasing parting with the railroads was all about. Freedom of movement in the land. Independence.

* * *

THE FIRST GLIDDEN TOUR, of 1904, ran all the way from New York to St. Louis. That was the year of the Fair. ("Meet me in St. Louis, Louis, Meet me at the fair . . .") The motorists were all amateurs, driving their own machines, and they had to cover at least seventy-five miles a day to get to St. Louis between July 25th and the 10th of August. For 1904 this was indeed an ambitious endurance run. Seventy-seven cars started, sixty-six finished. A 1,964 mile trip. No prizes were awarded that year, there were no rules. It was a case of come as you are, finish if you can, and have a dandy time while you're about it. Sounds like fun.

Jaspar Glidden was an enthusiastic motorist who had done a lot of driving in other parts of the world. Appalled by the condition of America's roads, the Glidden Tours were dreamed up by him—at least in part—to call attention to the sorry state of said highways and byways. The Glidden Tours received a lot of publicity. The sporting types who motored off into the boonies had a ripping time. Too bad Jaspar couldn't have left well enough alone. But, no, he had to go and offer an ornate loving cup for the 1905 run. A set of rules was established. In 1905 there would be a "winner." The pleasant jaunt of 1904 turned into a contest.

Percy Pierce in his 28 h.p. Pierce Great Arrow won the '05 Tour, which was a run from New York City to Bretton Woods, New Hampshire, and included a hill climb at Mt. Washington. One of the earliest female motorists took part in the '05 run. This was Jean Cuneo, who drove her White steamer off a bridge into a stream. Nobody was injured and her car was pulled and pushed back to the road. Plucky lass, she continued the Tour. Jean Cuneo went on to set track records and make a perfect score in the 1908 Glidden Tour. She was another woman who didn't care a rap that motoring was supposed to be a man's game.

The Glidden Tours ran every year from 1904 until 1913. The '09 Tour penetrated all the way to Denver, and the 1910 Tour ran from Cincinnati to Chicago via *Texas*, a trip of 2,851 miles, which turned out to be the longest of the Glidden Tours. The last Glidden Tour, of 1913, started in Minneapolis and ended at Glacier National Park, Montana. But by that time the event had become quite the prestigious endurance run, with manufacturers entering cars with factory drivers. The car manufacturers were the antithesis of the motoring sportsman. They wanted to *win*, to take the prized Glidden Trophy back to wherever they happened to be making their cars. Good for business, which was all that counted. Many of the cars were obviously put together

The Crystal Park Auto Road in about 1910. At left is one of the specially built, mountain-climbing Packards owned by the toll road company. At the end of the road the cars were placed on a large wooden turntable and turned around for the trip downhill. The other, toll-paying private autos serve as the backdrop for this de rigeur photo, to show the folks back home that the group made it.
Pikes Peak Library District

Another photo along the Crystal Park Auto Road, taken in 1910. The road was located near Colorado Springs. See the beginning of this chapter for another view along this route. **Pikes Peak Library District**

Pictured here at the wheel is Godfrey Sykes, a British scientist who settled in the Southwest to work and study. He was a motoring enthusiast who used automobiles for desert exploration. The car in this photo may be an EMF "30," a very good machine in its day.

Arizona Historical Society Library/Tucson

with the Glidden Tour in mind, and the manufacturers were at each other's throats, arguing about what constituted a stock car. The Glidden "Tour" became a contest beteen manufacturers, not exactly what Jaspar Glidden had envisioned, which was "to see what an automobile could do, not in the manner of speed but as a pleasure vehicle for touring over the roads over long distances of diversified country." The fun had gone out of the enterprise. Jaspar called it quits.

But by 1913 plenty of attention had been called to the state of the nation's roads. Photos were published showing Glidden tourers down to their wheel hubs in mud, fording rivers, rolling through clouds of dust. Many drivers became completely lost. Some cars were just shaken apart. It became increasingly apparent that something would have to be done about our roads; the Glidden Tour became an annual reminder. To that extent, at least, it served its purpose.

The surprising thing about the Tours, as far as the modern reader is concerned, is that so many of the cars completed them. Given the same road conditions, not all modern cars would complete a Glidden Tour.

To give some weight to the notion that many of those old cars were far better than we give them credit for, we can take a look at the 1907 Maxwell Model HB that took part in the '07 Tour. Before joining the Tour, the Maxwell won the Chicago Motor Club Reliability Trial. The next day the hood was sealed. The car then won two races, one in Peoria, the other in Chicago. Then it joined the Glidden Tour in Cleveland. By the time the car pulled up to the factory in Tarrytown, New York, it had been driven 4,778 miles with its hood sealed. That would be a lot of trouble-free motoring even today.

* * *

OH, THE AMERICANS weren't alone in dreaming up hairy-scary wilderness endurance runs for their motorists. The Peking-to-Paris race of 1907 reached a plateau of absurdity when it was discovered that no roads whatsoever existed in many parts of Asia. The drivers and mechanics had to disassemble their machines in order that local citizens could carry them piecemeal over a range of mountains.

Not satisfied with the 1907 race across Eurasia, *Le*

Matin and the New York *Times* sponsored the New York-to-Paris race of 1908, possibly the most famous of the early long distance endurance races. The New York-to-Paris race is too well known to discuss at length here. Books have been written about it, even a novel, and a movie was made of the event.

As many proud Americans know, if they know anything at all about the race, it was won by the Thomas Flyer, an American car. The race was won on total elapsed time, however, because a German car got to Paris first. The Americans won because of the good time they made across the United States . . . preceded by a rolling machine shop that was loaded with spare parts. The machine shop went by *rail* but was never for long out of touch with the cars. The Thomas Flyer pulled into San Francisco forty-two days out of New York. The other cars were hundreds of miles behind them.

The race was intended originally to continue across Alaska to the Bering Sea, then cross over on the ice. Well, in the first place, the Bering Sea might not ice over; and if it did, it certainly wasn't going to be a place to race a pack of automobiles. In the second place, there was no way to get automobiles across Alaska under their own power. The rules were changed then and the cars still in the race were shipped by boat to the Orient. The race continued from Vladivostok and the Germans won through first into Paris, the Americans just be-

hind, and the Italians last. Just three cars finished the race.

It had been a terrible trip. Accounts left by the men who completed the race tell of unbelievable hardships as they pushed through virgin automobile territory in Asia. Such a race was never again attempted.

* * *

BY 1910 we had plenty of automobiles scattered around the Rocky Mountain and desert regions of the United States. The area was becoming relatively civilized. Rainbow Bridge in Utah was discovered in 1909. Automobile tours along the rim of the Grand Canyon were a regular feature by 1910 (a Santa Fe railroad spur had been pushed through to the Grand Canyon in 1901). Up in Colorado Springs, flatlanders in town to escape the summer heat at home could rent cars to take them to the Garden of the Gods or wherever else the chauffeur or his boss dared let the car go. Motoring away from the railroads was becoming an acceptable diversion in even the most remote parts of the West by 1910, although long distance motoring was certainly not yet everybody's cup of tea. But one of the first motor tourists across the far reaches of the great Southwest was my old friend Harold Collyer, who, with a friend and a Model T roadster, struck out from his home in West Texas in 1910 to see California and the ocean.

On March 18, 1911, Teddy Roosevelt, out of office at the time, motored to Phoenix to dedicate the Roosevelt Dam. 280 feet high and 1,080 feet long, the dam was worthy of him.
Arizona Historical Society Library/Tucson

Somewhere west of Only God Knows Where, some citizens of the South-west push their car through deep sand. The trick was to keep up the momentum. Such strain was hard on the cars as well as the motorists.
Arizona Historical Society Library/Tucson

Where did he find the tree trunk? Mormon Lake, Arizona, in about 1917. One learned how to move a heavy, dead object with levers, an interesting study of physics if not of driving. Looks like this fellow has pulled off his muffler.
Arizona Historical Society Library/Tucson

2

The Tourist — Part One

AROLD COLLYER AND BUD PRICE were among the first "motor gypsies," "motor nomads," or "gasoline gypsies," as many of the camping motorists who traveled just prior to WWI were called. Harold was twenty and Bud about the same age. Their car wasn't new, but it couldn't have been very old either. In 1910 a new Model T still cost about $780. I don't know where they got the money to buy the car; Harold forgot to tell me. They were both farm-ranch boys, however, already skilled in keeping machinery running with baling wire, spit, and a few cuss words. Harold said he was glad he talked Bud into making the trip; Bud died in 1918 during the influenza epidemic and Harold said it was good he got to see something of the world besides West Texas.

The boys left home with five gallons of gasoline, five gallons of water, and a couple of gallons of oil tied to the running boards. They carried enough tools to open up a repair garage anyplace along the way. Shovel, axe, and camping gear were tied on. Spare tires and desert bags (drinking water) were attached wherever else they could find room. Full of bacon and biscuits, they chattered away from home on a cool morning.

It was still quite hot when they pulled into Deming, New Mexico, late that night, out of water, almost out of gasoline, and tired right down to the bone marrow from shoveling sand. The day had taught them one thing about desert travel: get an *early* start, even before the sun comes up; get down the road a ways before the day heats up. Relax in the middle of the day, if you have to. Travel again in the evening. Summertime in the Southwest is an unhealthy time of the year to be shoveling sand under the midday sun. They bought tarps to throw under the tires, for traction over soft sand.

Two or three days later they showed up in Tucson, where they had to replace a tire; sand and heat were already hard at work on the Ford. They drove through Gila and Yuma, places that have their own brand of summer heat. Harold never explained why he took that route, or why, if he had to go that way, he couldn't have gone at a better time of the year. If I had asked him, I'm sure he would have said something about West Texas boys not being strangers to heat. When they had to repair tires along the road, they tied the tarp to the car, staked the other end of the tarp to the ground, and worked in the shade. Harold might have said, too, that in the early days of motoring tourists and fools were likely to rush in to the same damn places.

After they crossed the Colorado River into California, they ran into deep sand. The Ford ground away through the sand, gulping water for relief. At last they came to the famous wooden road that had been put down over the dunes. (Reportedly, parts of it can still be sighted off the present highway.) The road was just wide enough for one car, but wider places had been built into the road every mile or so in order to let one car pass another. Harold and Bud didn't meet anybody.

The Globe-Phoenix Stage on the Globe-Phoenix (Arizona) Auto Road, about 1914. **Arizona Historical Society Library/Tucson**

The road to Bisbee, Arizona, in 1915. This looks to have been an automobile outing. **The Buehman Collection, Arizona Historical Society Library/Tucson**

When they fueled up in El Centro, they learned that the road over the hills to San Diego was so rough and steep that their T might not make it. Gasoline was fed to the T carb by gravity; going uphill, gas just might not feed to the carb properly if the road happened to be too steep. Some drivers solved the problem by *backing* uphill, but when you were climbing a steep, narrow, winding mountain road that climbed for several miles, such a tactic could prove impractical. Harold and Bud solved that problem by stationing Bud out on a fender with a can of gasoline. He poured gas into the carburetor at just the right intervals to keep the car going. It was a risky business because Bud was always in danger of falling off the car—it was a rough road—or accidentally pouring gasoline all over the engine and possibly

starting a fire that would destroy their car.

They pulled out on top at Jacumba, 4,000 feet above sea level and fifteen degrees cooler. It felt so good up there they decided to camp under a big tree while they worked on the car, cleaning it and greasing it, and going over it with their tools to tighten anything that had vibrated loose. This was a common chore with the early drivers. The cars vibrated a good bit all by themselves, but after bouncing all over bad roads for a week or so, they could be in need of tender attention with wrenches and screwdriver.

Arriving in San Diego, they camped near the seashore, fascinated by the big rollers that boomed in and filled the air with spray. When not busy down by the shore, they mounted two new tires. Then they decided

Opening day of Arizona's Superior to Miami Highway, 1918. This trip, now on a paved road, is still an exciting ride through rugged mountain terrain. **Arizona Historical Society Library/Tucson**

Prior to the First World War, a group of autos have climbed up and out of Arizona's Salt River Canyon. This is another impressive drive even today. **Arizona Historical Society Library/Tucson**

to head north. The sand was so deep that they had to let air out of the tires to give themselves better traction, a common remedy in those days for driving on sandy roads.

Long Beach proved to be another good stop. They were able to make a little money there, working in a garage, cleaning and greasing cars, changing oil and repairing tires. After a month in Long Beach, they packed their T and headed back east. The Model T was again clean and tight, all of its tires in good condition.

Harold and Bud decided to go by way of Needles, along the Santa Fe Railway, having learned that route should be preferable to the way they had come. As things turned out, it wasn't much of a choice, just a different form of torture. Bouncing along all alone in a stretch of desert, the T came to a sudden stop. It was getting dark so they made camp. The next morning they worked on the car, trying to find the source of the trouble. As the day wore on, the temps eased up to about 120 degrees. A few cars came by and the drivers all stopped to see if they could be of help. It was an unwritten rule of the road—camaraderie along the trail of the lonesome tourist—that one did stop if one spotted a motorist who might be in distress. At last they found the problem, a broken coil wire which they were able to repair easily and quickly.

(Many years later, it was still the custom to stop alongside a car on the Alaska Highway to see if the motorist had a problem he couldn't solve by himself. Gasoline and repair shops were probably farther apart along that road than they were even in the first years of motoring in the United States. Leaving a motorist stranded could be dangerous for him, considering the potential severity of the weather up there. I always heard that one *had* to stop, although I don't know that an official rule or law existed. We always did stop, and other drivers always stopped for us to see if we were okay. Traffic was so sparse it certainly wasn't much of a chore. Once we helped a man repair a tire, as he had already blown his only spare, and he didn't know how to get the tire off the wheel so that he could patch the inner tube. At another spot I can remember helping a man lower the transmission out of his Buick. People from the States who traveled on the Alaska Highway before it was paved just couldn't get it through their heads that their cars would not stay together at 65 mph over dirt and gravel roads.)

Harold and Bud managed to get to Needles, but not until after dark. They were so tired they decided to put up in a hotel. Rain fell during the night. The main road east of Needles became impassable, so it was decided they should make a detour through Vidal. They took a reading of the odometer before they started out, so they would know, in case of a breakdown (or a bog-down), which way they should start walking, towards Vidal or back to Needles.

Vidal lay seventy-five miles away. They drove through thirty miles of soft sand with almost totally deflated tires, adding water to the overheated Ford every few miles, shoveling sand when the need arose, putting down and picking up their tarps. They "worked" (it could hardly be called driving) on into the night. It was cooler at night, although picking out the obscure trail became increasingly difficult as their fatigue grew. They pulled into Vidal in the very early morning, only to find that water was scarce; they could

A head-on collision on what is probably Oracle Road in Tucson, just before WWI. One wonders how they managed to come together on this wide road; drivers haven't improved greatly since then. **Arizona Historical Society Library/Tucson**

get only a gallon, not very much for the thirsty Ford.

Continuing on, the boys drove down to the ferry landing at the Colorado River. The ride over to Parker, Arizona, cost them $1.50, Harold recalled; but the ferryman's wife, taking pity on them—they looked decidedly seedy after working through the desert all night—invited them to a breakfast feed of hot cakes and bacon and a lot of strong, black coffee. Refueled, rewatered and revictualed, Harold and Bud rattled away in the direction of Phoenix, which lay at the end of a sandy road that wound in and out of the cacti. They stayed over in one of the very early auto-camps, where motorists gathered in the evening to tell each other lies about themselves and their cars.

Two motorists repair tires near Roswell, New Mexico. **Rio Grande Historical Collections, New Mexico State University Library**

Then on via Globe, which route was thought to be the best. They replaced a tire in Globe. The rains started again. Unable to buy chains for the car, the boys bought about fifty feet of good rope. Using a common trick of the time, they tied one end of the rope to a spoke, then wound it onto the tire and wheel, threading it between the spokes, keeping it as tight as they could. Once the rope was wound all the way around the tire and wheel, it was tied again to another spoke. Voilà. Maybe not as good as chains, but not so bad if that's all you've got. In high spirits, they pulled out of Globe.

Five miles later they were forced to get off the road and make camp. It grew dark. The rain poured down. Water flowed by them on the road. Lightning crackled. Thunder shook the ground. Harold said that during that night he learned exactly what the beginning of the world was like. They lay huddled together under their wet blankets and the dripping tarp, eventually falling asleep.

They woke around two or three in the morning. Everything had changed. The rain had stopped and they could see stars between the racing clouds. Some moonlight lit up the terrain. Also, they could hear a loud rumbling and roaring close by, as if a train were rushing past them. They discovered an arroyo just a few feet from their camp. Water rushed down the arroyo, rolling boulders along with it, carrying brush along in the current. The arroyo was on the verge of overflowing. As daylight came on, the water in the arroyo dropped, leaving a dead cow below them.

By now the boys were just anxious to get out of such a dangerous place. When a Packard came plowing through the mud in the afternoon from the other direction, they decided to chance it themselves. They still had the rope tied around their wheels. They took the fan belt off so the fan would not drown the spark plugs with water should they get in too deep, and then they headed up the road, trying to stay in the tracks left by the Packard. They drove for miles on the flooded road, the water often over the running boards. At last they climbed out of the flooded area. They removed the ropes from the wheels and put the fan belt back on, hoping

This photograph is entitled "Federal Route 70," which would place its location in southeast New Mexico; since the road has a number, the photo was probably taken in the early 1920s. The car is a Model T Ford, demonstrating one of the "T's" great talents, the ability to twist. Federal Route 70 seems an ambitious name for this minimal trail. **Rio Grande Historical Collections, New Mexico State University Library**

they hadn't damaged the engine by getting it too overheated. A few miles later they came to a bridge that had been partly washed away. Stuck again.

The two boys sat there pondering the swaying bridge with the storm water rushing beneath it. Harold said it was Bud who figured what to do. One way or another, the bridge had to be fixed. They didn't have carpentry tools along, but they did have some pieces of the bridge to work with, as well as some driftwood they found strewn along the bank of the stream. They took the rope and *tied* the bridge back together. Then, tentatively, they pushed the Ford onto the swaying, sagging structure, Bud behind, Harold walking alongside, one hand inside on the wheel to steer it.

That obstacle behind them, they came to a stop again when they got to the Gila River. No bridge at all. Just a fifty-yard-wide muddy stream filled with roiling brown water. Well . . .

They cooked up some beans and coffee. It was pointless going back. They would just sit it out, wait for the water to drop. It was restful sitting there in the sun, staying dry. Two Indians on a wagon rolled up to the river in the afternoon. The Indians knew no English, but they did speak some Spanish, which Harold could speak tolerably well, having learned it from Mexican cowhands. A deal was struck for two silver dollars.

Harold and Bud used what little rope they had left to tie onto the wagon and stretch back to the axle of the Ford. Harold took off the fan belt again, but this time he also stopped up the oil inlet with a rag so that water would not get into the engine. With Bud driving and the two horses in front of the wagon pulling, they started across the Gila. The water rushed under the wagon but pushed on the side of the car. They reached the other side only with great difficulty; they came within a whisker of losing the T right there. Harold vowed he would

never again venture across the Southwest during the rainy season.

The rest of the trip was comparatively uneventful. Just steady driving through sand and dust and mud, fixing a flat now and then for a break in the routine. They drove through Lordsburg, Deming, Las Cruces, El Paso. And home. All the tires were worn out. The car had about five hundred new rattles. (It should be remembered that a lot of wood was used in car bodies before the 1930s, and especially in the arid Southwest, the bodies would loosen up.) But they just cleaned the car, ground the valves, tightened her up . . . and she was about as good as a T could ever get. If any one car can be said to have conquered North America, it was the Model T. Over fifteen million were built.

Harold Collyer's trip is a good example of what lay ahead of the motorist if he took it into his head to explore new territory. Motoring was an excellent way to see the country. You couldn't miss it. The country was liable to get all over you in a coating of dust or mud. You had to have courage and be resourceful. Even to the point of defying death on a swaying bridge over a muddy torrent. Suspense. That's what it was all about.

* * *

THE FEW ACCOUNTS we have by true tourists, the amateurs, are historically interesting. Not many people today would choose either the conveyance or the roads. That these early days of motoring seem so quaint to us now is a good indication of how accustomed we have become to our Interstates. As John Steinbeck predicted in *Travels With Charley*, it is now possible to drive all the way across the United States without seeing anything.

By 1910 the annual production of automobiles had reached 181,000 and the registration of cars was ap-

Near Roswell, New Mexico, a group of impressive horses, overcome by curiosity, study a newcomer to the range, a Model T. **Rio Grande Historical Collections, New Mexico State University Library**

proaching a half million. In 1900 we had only about 8,000 automobiles in the United States, so if progress can be measured by units of automobiles, we were making it. A few so-called automobile authorities even predicted that one day the United States might have as many as a million cars, but most straight thinking people couldn't believe it. A million automobiles! One car for every ninety people then in the country? Unthinkable. We didn't have that many people in the country who could afford a car. (In those days, a car was bought with *cash*. No banker in his right mind would think of loaning a person money to throw away on such a diminishing asset. Anything could happen to it.) No, surely the saturation point as far as automobiles were concerned would be reached long before a million cars could be built. New cars would then be made only to replace those that would be worn out by the folks who could truly afford them. The "saturation point" of automobile production was bandied about. It has not been a subject of conversation for many years.

Who would have thought in 1910 that just ten years later *annual* production of cars would approach *two* million, and in the same year almost a half million trucks would be built? Not a soul. By 1920 it may have been possible to get every single American into a motor vehicle at the same time.

The railroads reached their peak of expansion just prior to 1920, in about 1917. If the average citizen couldn't predict the overwhelming future proportions of the automobile industry and the alacrity with which Americans would join the motoring society, neither could the men who ran the railroads. At first the railroads promoted the notion of motor vehicle usage as a means for more long distance travelers to get to railroads. Considering the awful condition of the nation's roads, it never occurred to them that once the people were mounted in their own cars they might just keep

driving, right past the railroad station, right on over the horizon. Which is just what they did. Full speed ahead and damn the roads . . .

By 1910, the transcontinental record was down to ten days, set by five men driving day and night in a four-cylinder Reo touring car. This was, of course, yet another promotional stunt, but roads out yonder must have been improving considerably if an automobile now took just twice as long as a train to get across the country.

One interesting aspect of these first trips is that many of the driver-writers thought to keep such careful track of their expenses. At one time automobile owners could think of little else to talk about except the performance of their cars. Any family get-together was bound to find several men joined in seemingly interminable conversation about gasoline and tire mileage. For a good many years such absorbing discussions even eclipsed sports as a topic. A little boy could listen through the cigar smoke and learn at least twice as much about cars as he would ever have to know.

One Midwesterner revealed that in 1911 he drove 2,723 miles to Los Angeles in 1,067 hours of running time. He averaged 16.3 miles per hour (come to think of it, the roads couldn't have been so hot after all) and got almost 15 miles to the gallon (not so good either). He was driving a White, one of the more ubiquitous machines on the roads then. *Hundreds* of different marques were built between 1900 and 1920, many of them now just a name in a book, not even one example remaining. Estimates of the number of different makes produced in the United States varies between 2,000 and 3,000. At one time almost anybody who owned a machine shop was liable to build a few cars. In 1915 El Paso County, Colorado, had 1,472 cars registered, but this number included 115 different makes. Fords totaled 367 in the county, followed by Buick with 181,

A couple of the local girls in Carrizozo, New Mexico, mounted in their Model T and well prepared with a spare tire and a desert bag for water.
Rio Grande Historical Collections, New Mexico State University Library

The geology class at New Mexico State University set out in January of 1914 to prove that travel is educational. Three cars loaded with students met in front of the drugstore in Mesilla Park and set out for the Organ Mountains with well-filled lunch baskets. Although they had to climb hills and plow through sand and go through two or three deep arroyos, the students and instructors got all the way to the Modoc Mine, where they studied specimens. At a few points during the trip, the students had to get out of the cars to assist the machines. The day turned out well, and it was concluded that more field trips would be made as soon as the weather got warm enough for sleeping out. **Both, Rio Grande Historical Collections, New Mexico State University Library**

then in order of their numbers, Cadillac, Chalmers, E.M.F., Overland, Studebaker, Hudson, Maxwell, Baker Electric, Franklin, Hupmobile, Reo, and Packard.

* * *

SOONER OR LATER, *some*body had to notice how bad the roads were. In the second decade of the century, with more and more people depending on motor vehicles for their livelihood, some cries for help from the wilderness trail started to be heard even in the nation's capitals. Of course, by that time a few of the lawmakers and bureaucrats owned cars, so something was bound to happen. Up until the highway legislation of the second decade was passed, road building was generally in the hands of the counties. Now state government, with money partly from the federal government, stepped in. A good deal of this road building interest was inspired by the creation of the Lincoln Highway, although millions of Americans had a hard time getting excited about the idea of a comprehensive highway system as long as the railroads connected all the large cities. Many folks equated new roads with more taxes, which was of course the case; the railroads were supported by private enterprise.

The Lincoln Highway was dedicated on October 31,

1913, to connect the coasts with one road, from New York to San Francisco via Philadelphia, Pittsburgh, Chicago, Cedar Rapids, Omaha, Denver, Laramie, Salt Lake City, Ely, Reno, Sacramento, and Oakland. A solid red line all the way across the country. A red line, sure. A good road? No. The Lincoln "Highway" just showed the route of roads, trails—call them what you will—that already existed before the idea of the Lincoln Highway was dreamed up. The Highway received an impressive amount of advertising, but it was years before it would deserve to be called a highway. Some discovered it was just a direct route to disaster.

It's generally not realized that a good part of the Lincoln Highway was improved by private donations from people and companies in the automobile industry. The road could be good here, poor over there. Out west, where travelers were few and counties had little money for road improvements, a trip along the Lincoln Highway could be fraught with as much bitter surprise as on any other road in the country. The old Lincoln Highway route can still be followed today, but it's been a numbered road for decades. Lincoln's memorial road is just another anonymous route now.

* * *

Sitting by his fireside, a fellow could conjure up some romantic notions about motoring across America. Freed from the tyranny of railroad schedules. Out in the healthy open air, away from the sooty trains. On his own, doing for himself. Driving right down Main Street, not seeing the back end of every city, its dumps, junkyards, outhouses. Camping out, having picnic lunches under big old trees, away from the railroad hotel and its gastronomic horrors. Getting to *know* America. Load up the Tin Lizzie and go.

Recommended cross-country equipment: axe, shovel, coffee pot, desert water bags, canned food to last several days, some blankets and tent or tarp, block and tackle, a good length of rope, tools, tarps or planks to lay down over mud or sand, spare parts (spark plugs, fuel pump, water pump, hoses, fan belt) tires and tubes, maps, guide books, and a firearm. And plenty of money. Loaded as if for a safari, one still had to find room for the wife and kids.

A Mr. Bellamy, traveling out west in 1912, would not have believed the road over the Rockies was passable had he not seen the tire tracks ahead of him. He was driving a Matheson, one of our better cars, which could have cost him as much as $3,000. The road was washed away so deeply in places he had to stop to rebuild the road now and then. Making a rapid turn in one of the washes, his car skidded sideways and then took a nosedive into a gully. It was the next day before another traveler came along the road, a ranch wagon being pulled by some terrified mules that had never before seen an automobile. Bellamy was pulled out and he managed to plow onward to the next town where his damaged car could be repaired.

In 1915, driving all alone in a Stutz Bearcat, a daredevil by the name of Cannonball Baker roared across the country in eleven days, seven hours, and fifteen minutes, a new record for the solo driver. The Bearcat was one of the few true sports cars ever made in this country. Cannonball tied down the rear springs and removed the fenders, transforming his street machine into the closest thing resembling a race car that a man could buy from a factory.

* * *

While Cannonball was hurtling west to east in his Stutz, another traveler was wending her way toward San Francisco from New York in one of the more inappropriate machines ever to take on the wilderness. Luckily for the lady, she didn't meet Cannonball, because she had problems enough.

The lady—and we can certainly assume she was a Lady—was Emily Post, the very same social arbiter who standardized behavior for generations with her book *Etiquette*, published in 1922. Thank heavens she survived the trip.

Emily Post and her son Edwin . . . and all of the luggage they decided they would need for a transcontinental trip.

Emily Post, E. P. Dutton Collection

Edwin Post, Jr., and his magnificent Mercedes in the Great Southwest. Close inspection of the photo does not reveal a road.
Emily Post, E. P. Dutton Collection

Like many Easterners of the day, Emily knew a good deal more about Europe than she did about the United States. She and her friends could have been counted among those Americans who believed that civilization, insofar as it existed at all in the United States, ended at the Hudson River. They spent their summers in Europe. Emily had traveled by automobile in Europe, way back in '98 when she experienced a motor trip from the Baltic to the Adriatic. But summers in Europe ended in 1914. The war that ended the world as far as Emily and her generation had come to know it raged on and on.

She decided she would like to see the Pan-American Exposition of 1915 in San Francisco, and she also thought there could be no more charming way of getting there than by automobile. Was she thinking of her

trips around Europe? Well, there it was, New York to San Francisco by car. Her friends scoffed. After all, once one left New York or San Francisco by train, there was absolutely nothing to see. Why bother going by car? Take a train. Sleep all the way.

But Emily wasn't short on spunk. She put the idea to her son, Edwin M. Post, Jr., who was attending college in New England. He owned a perfectly magnificent machine, a Mercedes with an engine hood almost as long as a Model T. A wizard notion, Edwin decided. So they bought six new tires and a speedometer, topped off the oil and gasoline, loaded a good deal of luggage and a picnic basket filled with delicacies aboard the car, and headed out. They were accompanied by a female relative who is little mentioned in the book *Emily Post*

Edwin's Mercedes was a right-hand drive. Emily is well bundled up against the rigors of touring car travel.
Emily Post, E. P. Dutton Collection

wrote, *By Motor to the Golden Gate.*

Emily's trip is interesting from the point of view that she is somebody we know. Except for a burned-out bearing in New York and a little mud in Illinois, they had no real idea of what they were getting into until they got to Iowa. Then they learned what mud was all about. A lot of it covered the Lincoln Highway.

(Iowa and mud seem to go together in many accounts of early motoring. If even half of what we hear about Iowa and her roads was true, we can thank the gods of motoring that the folks there finally got around to paving their roads. One old party they met in the Midwest, when hearing they were considering shipping their car on by rail, said, "If that car was mine, I'd go right on plumb across Hell itself." Bucked up a bit, the Easterners continued on into the wide-open spaces.)

It became apparent to them that as splendid as the Mercedes might be in many respects, it was not built for wilderness trekking. It had a 144-inch wheelbase and a road clearance of but eight inches, with the exhaust pipe hanging very close to the ground. Climbing mountains, it proved tough to get the Mercedes around the turns. They would have to back and fill several times, the wheels at the edge of eternity. The exhaust pipe hung up on rocks and ruts so often that they finally shipped it on ahead by rail. Edwin said later that an American car, preferably a common make, would have been a more sensible vehicle for the trip. The Mercedes had been designed for the boulevards of Europe, not the mountain or desert roads of 1915 America. Even the tires were wrong; too narrow, they sunk easily in mud and sand under the heavy Mercedes.

The Post expedition rolled into Colorado Springs and paused in that social oasis until they had all revived their spirits. Friends still warned them off the trip. The hard part lay ahead. It could be dangerous; drunks or bandits might kill them. If nothing else, the idea seemed so boring and dreary. All that dirt. The terrible hotels and the abominable food. Think of it! Moving west by automobile, one did have to mix with the natives.

To be sure, the food and hotel rooms along the way were not quite up to the Ritz or the Biltmore, but Emily found most of the hotels reasonably clean, the grub at least edible. For the most part, the Posts tried to win through each day to a good hotel, but they didn't always make it. Most of the hotels in most of the towns in the West were still associated with train traffic. Located just across the street from the railroad depots, they were havens for commercial travelers. Such establishments were remarkable masculine lairs with well-used brass spitoons placed wherever a patron might have reason to pause, even in the dining rooms. Billiard rooms and bars could be located just off the lobbies, which were generally blue with drifting cigar smoke. Men lounged, read newspapers, chewed, smoked. Fading Victorian furniture stood on worn carpets.

Generally speaking, those old hotels had been furnished just once, as soon as they were built, which was right after the railroad passed through the town, about a generation before Emily Post arrived. They were hot

and musty summers, cold and drafty winters. Still, they were all that was available, and Emily found them a darned sight preferable to camping out on the prairie, which she was forced to do just once.

The beds in the rooms were brass, the springs squeaky. Once Emily lay wrapped in her coat all night, fighting bedbugs. A chair, chest of drawers, and a mirror completed the furniture. The room was also outfitted with a jug of water, a wash basin, hand towels and a Gideon Bible. Cleanliness from hotel to hotel was always a roll of the dice, except for the Harvey Houses along the Santa Fe, which were uniformly good.

The Posts forded their first stream, the Huerfano River, in southern Colorado, and they got used to the practice as they pushed across New Mexico. Edwin did say that in his opinion a shovel should not be necessary east of New Mexico. Don't, Edwin cautioned, venture into a stream that is so deep it might cover the carburetor. An Englishman who was just ahead of them at one point did this. The man's valet had already waded into the stream and declared it only knee-deep and with a firm, pebbly bottom. The Britisher splashed his car into the stream . . . and down, down until water was sucked into the carb. The cylinder heads exploded most distressingly right off the engine. It had been quite a valuable machine.

Edwin tells us that once you get your car into a stream, stay in first gear until you get to the other side. Go through at a constant speed, because it is easier to keep going than to try to pick up forward momentum again. In mud or sand, change to a lower gear and keep going. Keep going. That's right. Edwin learned a few things they couldn't teach him in college.

Edwin doesn't mention crossing arroyos, but crossing them was inevitable in the Southwest. Only deep streams that always carried water were bridged. Arroyos were not bridged. The drivers liked to hit the bottom in second gear, churn across the sand, shift quickly into low at the far side of the arroyo, and pull up and out. The secret was to not miss first gear.

The Great Void. This is the track Emily and Edwin Post had to follow as they crossed the prairie.

Emily Post, E. P. Dutton Collection

The Posts crossed the Southwest in the spring when the roads were still somewhat rutted from the past winter's traffic, before summer rains could turn the roads to mud again, before the rains might fill the arroyos. Very often arroyos have to be passed one after another. A traveler could be stuck between them for days if the weather continued bad. Luckily for the Posts, they passed through the Southwest before the Indians started their annual rain dances.

Emily and Edwin left New York without *Blue Books* to guide them. The 1915 edition wasn't ready. Someplace along the line they did acquire a *Blue Book*, at least for the Southwest, because she mentions using it. In fact, finding one's way across the Southwest without some kind of guide was impossible. One would inevitably get lost. Trails crossed in the middle of a great void; there was no farmer's house just across the road where one might ask directions and get a bucket of water. No signs, no farmers, no water.

One traveler recalled asking direction of an Indian. The motorist pointed down the road and asked if that might be the way. The Indian nodded. Then, before taking off, the driver thought to ask if his destination lay in the opposite direction. He pointed back down the trail. The Indian nodded again. Then the paleface driver pointed all around the horizon, the Indian nodding as fast as he could. As it turned out, the Indian did not speak English.

On the other hand, many motorists were guided across the Southwest by Indians or cowboys on horseback, the horses walking slowly in front, the cars chattering along behind, until the correct trail could be pointed out to the dudes.

The *Blue Books* were absolutely vital to the first motorists. Without numbered roads, with few direction signs posted, a stranger was lost. In any event, wooden signs in the West were likely to disappear, taken home for kindling by local citizens.

Yes, for motor touring one did need a *Blue Book*. The *Automobile Blue Book* was first published in 1901, and by 1915 there were eight volumes to cover the entire country. In fact, Emily would have needed six *Blue Books* to guide them all the way from New York to San Francisco.

The *Blue Book* gave directions about how to get from town to town. It was spiced with foldout maps, historical information, and photographs of raw roads and raw nature. Hotels, garages, and tire companies advertised in the *Blue Books*. Hotel rooms in Emily Post's day ran from $1.00 for a single to $4.00 for a double. The Hotel Medford, in Oregon, had a private phone in every room and "superb" cuisine. "Tourists linger longer till they can no longer linger," the folks at the Hotel Medford wrote.

Welding springs was a specialty of many garages, according to the *Blue Books*. One could order La Vake's Automobile Puller for $15, a device for pulling cars out of mud, sand, or snow. "A small boy can extricate the heaviest car." La Vake's Automobile Puller weighed 40 pounds, so one wonders just how small that boy was. Another outfit used for getting the old flivver out of a bog was the Pillsbury Hubpull. With the rear wheels turning, the line was pulled over the Hubpull and—theoretically—the car was moved out of the mess it had gotten itself into. The Hubpull cost $6.00. Looks dangerous.

Emily Post's automobile trip came to an end in Winslow, Arizona, so let's take a look at the *Blue Book* directions for the last part of Route 631, the trail from Springerville, Arizona, to Winslow. She joined the main road here after having driven the less desirable road through Gallup and Grants from Albuquerque. She had wanted to see the Painted Desert and the Indian pueblos at Acoma and Laguna.

They arrived at Holbrook, 98.7 miles west of Springerville:

"... town is across the river and to right. For Winslow, keep straight ahead on built-up road along river.

100.7 (total mileage from Springerville) Turn left with road. Turn right with road 101.2. Cross rough rocky place 102.0.

102.1 Fork, sign on left; bear left away from fence, following road across prairie. Pass windmill on right 109.1, running along fence for about 3 miles.

114.0 Curve left into road from right at sign. Cross short level flat 117.4; cross iron bridge over deep scenic canyon and stream 120.9, running upgrade just beyond.

121.1 Fork at top of grade; keep left, going straight ahead for several miles.

127.7 Curve right into prominent road from left. Cross long iron bridge over canyon 129.5.

133.2 Fork; bear left with travel.

138.8 Diagonal cross-road; bear left.

134.0 At high tank curve left along RR.

134.2 Right-hand street; turn right along elevated boardwalk.

134.3 WINSLOW, sta. on left."

Which is just what Edwin and Emily were looking for at that point, the railroad station. They had not been frightened by anything until they got to New Mexico, but by the time they reached Winslow, Arizona, Edwin had had it. So had the Mercedes, which by the way, featured elegant English coachwork. It cost them $151.20 to ship their two-ton car to Los Angeles on the Santa Fe. Emily was relieved to get aboard the train. She hadn't made it all the way by car, but she deserved a big hand for getting as far as she did.

As handy as the *Blue Books* were, they did have their limitations. It's easy to see that one should preferably have a companion along, reading the book, checking the mileage. Still, if said fence or said windmill had

An advertisement from a 1917 Blue Book. **Albert Manchester Collection**

Emily poses on the Staked Plains. **Emily Post, E. P. Dutton Collection**

Wagon trails often paralleled auto trails. This is 1915, probably in Colorado; Emily photographed the meeting of the new and the old.
Emily Post, E. P. Dutton Collection

disappeared during the interval between the time the trail blazer had passed and the motorist happened by, well, the tourist might have kept right on rolling into the vast beyond, never to be seen again . . .

* * *

IN 1913, when H. Brown drove his Buick to the top of Pikes Peak, the trip took him all day on an old carriage road. Brown broke some wheel spokes and his crankcase. Just three years later, on Labor Day 1916, the high ridges resounded with the roar and snarl of powerful cars. Clouds of dust drifted away from many curves as men and machines raced against time to the top. Barney Oldfield was there, chomping his cigar, but he wasn't making good time. It didn't matter, Barney's presence was all that was required to call attention to the new road, "the highest auto road in the world." Ray Lentz, of Seattle, won that first Pikes Peak Hill Climb, pushing his Romano Special twelve and a half miles up the narrow dirt road in only twenty minutes and fifty-five seconds.

Some changes had taken place on the mountain since Brown's 1913 trip and Ray Lentz's win in 1916. Most of those changes were due to Spencer Penrose, an expansive tycoon from Colorado Springs. The road to the top of Pikes Peak was built during the summer and fall of 1915. The road, which was estimated would cost

$25,000, ended up costing Penrose almost a quarter of a million dollars. The Pikes Peak Highway starts at 7,415 feet above sea level and climbs another 6,746 feet in twenty miles. The road was just seventeen miles long in 1916.

Spencer Penrose thought the auto road would draw attention to Colorado Springs. The Lincoln Highway passed through Colorado, and even in 1913 the road was drawing some motorists into the West. The new mountain road, opened with the presence of Barney Oldfield, was of course a success, another of Penrose's gambles that paid off, for himself and for Colorado Springs.

* * *

WITH ALMOST three and a half million automobiles rattling over America's terrible roads in 1916, the politicians started catching plenty of flak about doing something to help out the nation's motorists. Washington's answer, in 1916, was the Federal Aid Road Act, which appropriated $75,000,000 to go half-and-half with any state that agreed to build and maintain rural post roads. Although this was a good idea, it was the eastern states that got the most help; most of the eastern states had the other half of the money to put up, many western states did not. Western states were at least ninety percent rural, with sparse populations;

The Pikes Peak Highway

A White truck on Pikes Peak during construction of the Pikes Peak Highway. **Broadmoor Hotel**

A White Six just below the construction camp in 1916, after the road up Pikes Peak was constructed. **Pikes Peak Library District**

Looking down from Pikes Peak prior to WWI, the difficulty of the climb is apparent. The vehicle looks like a White gasoline-powered machine.
Pikes Peak Library District

Two White Sixes on Pikes Peak Highway, not long after the road to the top of the mountain was opened. The cars are similar, except the one on the right has a thermometer radiator cap, an after-market addition. Just about the time your radiator boiled over, these thermometers would tell you that the water was getting hot—but they sure looked snazzy. **Pikes Peak Library District**

they didn't have enough nickels to match Uncle Sam's. But even if they did put up some money, a western state would be so vast that road building money could disappear before the road had gotten anyplace. The mileage between towns in the West is very often greater than the distance across entire states in the East.

The Westerners were not ignorant, however, of the fact that most of the trails across their territory could hardly be considered automobile roads. In 1913, just a year after New Mexico became a state, the legislature authorized a $500,000 bond issue to assist the counties in road building and improvement. But not until 1919 was the New Mexico state government empowered to deal with the federal government over the building of highways. Until then, the roads in the state continued not much better than they had been in 1845, when

General Kearny, commanding the Army of the West, rode into Raton and told the people they had been Mexicans long enough.

* * *

THE MANUFACTURE and distribution of gasoline grew apace with the automobile. From being a waste product of the production of kerosene, gasoline soon had to be made for itself, and methods were developed, using heat and pressure, to get more gasoline out of each barrel of crude. Except in still remote places, gasoline was no longer sold by the can from general merchandise stores. Very early in the motoring game, a fellow could have a barrel of the stuff in his own garage, said barrel to be replenished on order by a local oil company. This custom must have provided the fire departments around

One of the earliest filling stations, this one is in Houston in 1916. The gasoline was in wheeled carts and could be trundled out to the curb.
Texaco

the country a good bit of activity.

The repair garages that were springing up all over also sold gasoline, but they did not always have pumps outside. Some garages had gasoline in wheeled carts that could be trundled out to the sidewalk, but a mechanic would have to be called from his work—not always with what could be called alacrity—to serve the gasoline customer. Or the motorist might have to drive into the garage—dark, cluttered places—and on down to the back someplace, wending his way between cars, mechanics, and other motorists, an often frightening experience for the timid driver.

The solution to all of this was, of course, the "filling station," and the first drive-in, off the road, off the sidewalk real live filling station seems to have appeared in Seattle, way back in 1907. By 1915 St. Louis had about thirty-five installations that could be called filling stations, businesses set up primarily to sell gasoline and other oil products, where repairs were incidental. Such a large number of filling stations in one town gives us a firm idea as to how early the automobile became a common part of the American scene. Oil companies

Looking south from the top of La Bajada (the descent just south of Santa Fe, New Mexico). This descent was approached with some trepidation by early drivers, especially flatlander dudes. The road dropped about a thousand feet in a short distance, with 23 switchbacks, curves and hairpin turns; a change in temperature was quite noticeable. **Museum of New Mexico**

started handing out free road maps in about 1914. Out west, a driver would still have to open cattle gates as he drove from town to town.

* * *

AMERICANS REVELED in this newly-discovered feeling of freedom as they deserted the railroads, even if they did have to stop and get out to open gates. Many drivers deserted the hotels, too, and so camping out in the "wilderness" with one's car became another national passion that has not cooled. At first, travelers simply stopped wherever they were when evening came on, much to the discomfiture of farmers who had to clean up after them. But soon enough many towns set aside an area for campers, and here, at the end of grueling days, the motorists gathered. The camping areas were often free—or next door to it—and such places were handy to town shops. Mornings, the townspeople could stroll by to sneak glimpses of the strangers going through their ablutions. Town motorist's camps developed into state camping parks—away from the towns—and some local citizens started putting up a few "tourist

cabins" if they happened to have space next to the house. Such cabins can still be spotted in the United States, in the older parts of the country, a line of three or four sagging, weathered structures, often with small porches attached, behind or beside abandoned farms, or at the edge of small towns now bypassed by the interstates.

Surely a study could be made of the effects of the automobile on the commercial traveler . . . the drummer—today's traveling salesman. Before the automobile came along, a drummer would ride the train, catch it in one town, get off in the next where he hoped to get orders. But after completing his business, he was stuck there until another train came by, which could be the next day. He could drink beer and shoot pool with the yokels. But he couldn't get on to the next town, which might be thirty or forty miles away. The automobile gave him more range. Now a fellow could bother customers in three or four towns in one day, pick up many more orders than ever before. It seems likely that the automobile, which was one of the main reasons for the rapid growth of heavy industry in general in the first decades of the century, was also responsible for the growth of many industries not directly related to it, simply because company representatives could cover so much more territory in a given amount of time if they were mounted on their own wheels.

Motorized salesmen started penetrating the most remote parts of the country, wherever they had customers, just as long as they could discern a trail heading in the right direction. Commercial travelers were among the earliest long-distance motorists in the Far West.

On the 8th of March, 1916, a traveling salesman from Albuquerque by the name of Walter Staley finished his work in Deming earlier than expected. He sold hardware of various kinds for several different companies. Since he still had plenty of daylight, he decided to drive on down to Columbus in his Maxwell tourer. Columbus was only thirty or so miles away. With a little luck and no tire trouble, he would get down there before dark, have supper and get to bed early. He planned to get up with the sun, finish his work, and get on the road before noon. He hoped to be in El Paso before dark the next day.

Staley put up at a hotel in Columbus. But he was awakened a lot earlier than he had expected to be, and the next time he saw his Maxwell it was burned out and full of bullet holes.

A section of the original La Bajada as it appeared in 1981. A new La Bajada has been built about half a mile to the east which is neither as scary nor as interesting as the old.
Albert Manchester

The depot at Columbus, New Mexico, as it appeared at the time of Pancho Villa's raid. "Elevation 4062 feet, to El Paso 73 miles." Below, downtown Columbus, New Mexico, the day after Pancho Villa's raid. **Above, David Myrick Collection; below, Rio Grande Historical Collections, New Mexico State University Library**

War: Wheels Across the Border

"Three exciting events took place during my sojourn at Columbus (New Mexico). First, the 'Golden State' (a train) passed through every day going east. This occurrence was attended regularly by all present for duty. Second, the 'Golden State' passed through every day going west. This was attended also by all present for duty. Third, Villa raided the camp and town on March 9, 1916. This, likewise, was attended by all those present for duty."

Lt. John P. Lucas, 13th Cavalry

The Southern Pacific Railroad's famous Golden State *passed through Columbus every day, once going east, once going west. Many of the troops stationed in town turned out to see it; excitement was hard to come by in Columbus.*

Columbus Historical Society

BULLET STOPPED the clock in the railroad station at Columbus at 4:11 on the morning of March 9th. It was a cold morning, although at the time the bullet cracked through the railroad station window and then stopped the clock, Columbus was the hottest place on the continent, suffering through its only rendezvous with history, one spark of violence in the vast, black, otherwise silent desert. Hundreds of Pancho Villa's tough irregulars shot it out with some equally tough U.S. cavalry troopers and a lot of frightened U.S. citizens.

Flames from torched hotels and stores in the center of town lit up the bullet-whipped streets. Machine guns roared. Rifles and pistols cracked. Angry, desperate men darted through shadows and the flickering light from the fires. Out on the street in front of the hotel, the bullet-pocked car of the traveling salesman burst into flames as its gasoline tank ignited . . .

Columbus is a remote border town thirty-five miles south of Deming, New Mexico, and the present I-10. Mexico, in the shape of Palomas, Chihuahua, lies just three miles farther down the road. Today, Columbus may have fewer residents than the 400 who lived there in 1916, and at that time 350 officers and men of the 13th Cavalry Regiment were stationed at Camp Furlong, which lay just south of the east-west Southern Pacific railway line. A few of the camp buildings remain. The crossties and tracks are now gone from the railroad bed. The railroad station is still there, now a local museum in commemoration of Columbus' few months of fame.

Part of Camp Furlong has been transformed into Pancho Villa State Park, where a passing traveler can put down stakes right next to what used to be the Adjutant General's Office. The corrugated tin roofs of the eroding adobe buildings rattle in the vagrant desert winds. A fragment of wall still stands of the quarters from which Lt. Lucas, barefoot and with pistol in hand, sallied into a night of fighting. A cactus garden spreads over the sides of Cootes Hill, which also figured in the battle; the DO NOT TOUCH THE PLANTS signs along the trails through the garden seem like an unnecessary admonishment. A plaque set among the cacti advises the traveler that Pancho Villa's raid was the last time the United States was invaded by foreign troops.

The "invasion" lasted at the most six hours, not much of an invasion as those things go in this century. The "foreign troops" were Villa's guerrilla fighters, and Villa was in revolt against the de facto government of Venustiano Carranza. The history on the plaque, like so many aspects of the raid and the resulting "punitive expedition," has become distorted through the years.

Why did Pancho Villa attack Columbus?

For one of several reasons or a combination of reasons. The raid could have been to acquire arms, ammunition, food, and—so important to Villa's style of warfare—good horses. Or he may have crossed the border to get arms and ammunition from Sam and Louis Ravel, storekeepers who had already received money from him. Or the incursion may have been for revenge:

Woodrow Wilson had recognized the Carranza regime, an act that kindled Villa's short fuse; and Wilson had allowed Carranzista troops to pass through the United States on a train to reinforce the Mexican federal garrison at Agua Prieta. The Carranzista generals, having learned a few tricks from the war in Europe, caused Villa to waste his vaunted *división del norte* on barbed wire, trenches, and machine guns at Agua Prieta.

The courage of Villa's men and the weight of the rampant cavalry charge were no longer enough; the "art" of warfare had passed Villa's limited capacity to deal with it; he was, first and last, a hit-and-run guerrilla fighter. He was hurting and angry as his force limped toward Columbus. Compared to the raped towns and villages of Mexico, Columbus must have looked like Fat City, and possibly not a nut too tough for his boys to crack. Most likely he was thinking about killing two birds with one stone: embarrass the Carranza regime by showing the gringos the Mexican government had no control in the north and steal the arms, food, and horses he needed.

U.S. intelligence placed Villa in the area, or approaching, but nobody realized he was as close as he was, and few imagined that he would even think of attacking across the border. If the U.S. Army was in a fog where Villa was concerned, the Mexican did not have the same problem as far as the situation at Columbus and Camp Furlong was concerned. It is now felt that Villa had spies in Columbus and that he had planned the raid for quite some time. In any event, while Villa and about 485 of his men crossed the border west of town, the soldiers of Camp Furlong and the citizens of Columbus went to bed as usual. The people in

The regimental Headquarters building at Columbus. It is in what is now called Pancho Villa State Park, where one can picnic or camp. This is an adobe structure, the adobe bricks set in with concrete. The adobes have eroded; the concrete didn't.
Albert Manchester

Memorial services being held at Columbus for the victims of Pancho Villa's raid of March 9, 1916. Even at this early date, the automobile was becoming a prominent part of this community.
Museum of New Mexico

the scattered frame and adobe dwellings lay sleeping. The center of town was silent and dark. Two columns of Villistas crept forward, one column advancing into town along the railroad tracks, the other infiltrating the cavalry post. A detachment of Mexicans occupied Cootes Hill. The attack was probably meant to envelope the gringos, hit everyplace and all at once. Surprise. Pancho Villa had been practicing for a long time.

If the surprise was complete, the response of the U.S. Cavalry troopers at the post and many of the citizens in town was also a surprise, as far as Villa and his men were concerned. The battle stuttered to life as cavalry sentinels discovered the Mexicans in their midst. No-quarter fights erupted all over Columbus and Camp Furlong. Gringo resistance was immediate and extraordinarily lethal. The average frontier American of the day was pretty handy with the weapons most of them kept. They were not unarmed Mexican villagers. And the U.S. Cavalry was considered *the* elite unit of the Army, "twice as small and twice as tough as any other unit," disciplined and well trained. Although it was very early in the morning, between 3:30 and 4:00, the cook shack was already in business. When the Villistas tried to force their way in, they were beaten off with boiling water, potato mashers, axes, anything the cooks could lay their hands on. Individuals in town, routed into the cold morning by gunfire, responded in kind.

Cavalry officers and noncoms organized the troopers and pushed across the tracks into town. Fires broke out there as the raiders torched hotels and stores. The Mexicans raged through the streets, bent on mayhem. The U.S. Cavalry troopers lurked in the shadows and returned accurate rifle fire. Out at the post, other cavalry troopers fought back to save their lives and their precious cavalry mounts. The confused battle was staged in the light of the flickering flames.

Narrow escapes were as common as rattlesnakes that night. A.B. Frost tried to drive out of town with his wife and baby in the family car. Frost was hit by a bullet before he could get very far, so his wife, a capable lady of the West, pushed him into the back seat and continued their escape through the crossfire. One family, hiding in the brush outside their house, was discovered by a lone Villista. They put him down with a shotgun blast, then bashed his head in. Residents of a hotel were pulled out of their rooms and killed. Out in the streets, cavalry troopers gunned down anybody in a big sombrero.

Whatever Villa expected to find in Columbus, it certainly wasn't the slaughter of his own men. As dawn approached, he decided to pull out while he still could. Mexican bugles sounded recall. The Villistas crept out of town, mounted up, and raced across the border, some of them herding a few U.S. Cavalry mounts with them, others carrying whatever small bits of loot they could.

General John J. "Black Jack" Pershing in Columbus, New Mexico, getting ready to return to the field south of the border. The staff car looks like a 1916 Buick tourer; note the rifle butts poking up in the rear seat.

Museum of New Mexico

Right behind them galloped over thirty troopers of the 13th Cavalry in very hot pursuit. The troopers would dismount and fire, then mount and chase the Mexicans until they were close enough for another shot. And so the chase went for fifteen miles into Mexico, until the Mexicans, realizing how few gringos were at their heels, turned to fight. Outnumbered, their horses exhausted, the cavalry troopers retired across the border, counting dozens of raiders they had dropped in the mesquite during the running fight. This was in the days when firepower meant marksmanship, when the '03 Springfield with its .30-06 cartridge was arguably the best military rifle in the world.

South of the border in August of 1916, a traveler went well armed. Here a sergeant of cavalry accompanies a scout who remembered to bring his raincoat as well as two belts of rifle ammunition.

Columbus Historical Society

* * *

COLUMBUS WAS A SHAMBLES. A farmer, driving milk to town that morning, saw smoke rising in the still air. At first he thought there had been just a bad fire . . . until he started to meet refugees from town.

At least seventy dead Mexican raiders littered the streets (not very many prisoners were taken). Eighteen dead and eight wounded U.S. citizens and soldiers were gathered up. In terms of casualties, the raid was a disaster for Villa. While telegraph messages clattered back and forth along the border and to Washington, D.C., men of the 13th Cavalry carried the dead Mexicans out of town and burned them on piles of old railroad ties. Another column of smoke rose in the sky over Columbus.

But the Americans were hurt too. The raid on Columbus was neither the first nor the last time that armed Mexicans passed north of the border during the 1910-1920 period that Mexico was out of control, but the blatancy of the attack was too much even for Woodrow Wilson. The high cost in lives and property was not passed over with a flurry of diplomatic letters. The determinedly pacific Wilson was now fighting mad. Major General John "Black Jack" Pershing was ordered to take a force across the border to find, disperse, and destroy Pancho Villa's outfit. On March 15th, 1916, columns of cavalry, supported by infantry and artillery, rode into Mexico, the sun in their eyes, grit in their teeth. The fighting horse cavalry of the U.S. Army was off on its last campaign. One of its toughest.

An old Mexican song, a *corrido*, tells how Pancho Villa flew in an airplane high above the desert and mountains of Chihuahua, looking down at the bumbling gringo soldiers who were wandering impotently through the wilderness. According to legend, Villa easily outwitted and outran the heavily laden U.S. cavalrymen. That's how the story almost invariably goes on both sides of the border, a story reinforced by Mexican pride, our own ignorance about what our soldiers accomplished there, and our willingness to believe in the ineptitude of our military men.

That version of the story is wrong. Pitifully small by European standards (about 100,000 men, 15,000 of them in the cavalry), poor in most modern equipment, the U.S. Army, such as it was, was ready for action. The border country was still a bloody frontier; the cavalrymen kept themselves, their mounts, their weapons finely tuned.

E.A. Capen, Major of Cavalry, Retired, was only twenty-two when he jogged off into Mexico with the 6th Cavalry. He had been in the cavalry since 1913. He now lives in Weslaco, Texas, and he recalls the campaign with incredible clarity. Trooper Capen and his comrades were armed with sabers (a model designed by George Patton), Springfield rifles, and the Colt .45 semiautomatic pistol. Their mounts carried, besides tack and rider, the trooper's weapons, 200 or more rounds of ammunition, several days of field rations for trooper and mount, mess gear, water, changes of clothing and an overcoat, blanket, shelter half, picket pins, extra horseshoes, grooming tools, and toilet kit. So loaded, a cavalry mount was expected to march thirty miles a day, or sixty miles or more in the event of a forced march. One can see then why the Army did not look for *big* men to ride its horses. Nevertheless, a cavalry horse could be carrying a load of over 250 pounds.

The average cavalry mount of the latter days of the cavalry was generally half Thoroughbred, half nondescript range horse, although many cavalrymen liked a bit of Morgan or Arabian blood mixed in. The mounts were geldings (most mares were too small), were 14-2 to 15-2 hands high, possibly up to 16 hands, and weighed 1,000 to 1,200 pounds. This cavalry horse was developed in the first decade of the century under the Remount Program; the Punitive Expedition was its first real test in the field. The troopers who were assigned the mounts took care of them before they tended to their own needs ("Boy, the Army can always find another soldier, a horse costs us $150."). The cavalrymen were youthful adventure-seekers like Trooper Capen or the flotsam and jetsam of society. But the cavalry was only half man; the other half was horse, and the horses they rode into Mexico proved to be worthy comrades.

The Punitive Expedition was not one long column of cavalry, infantry, artillery, and escort wagons stumbling, rattling, clattering through Chihuahua at the base of a slow-moving cloud of dust. The Punitive Expedition was, at first, several "flying columns" made up of a hundred or more cavalrymen (two or more troops), loaded with ammo, hardtack, bacon, coffee and oats, and let loose into the countryside, ranging far and fast, wherever the troop leader had an inkling he might be able to trap Villa or some of his boys.

During its first month in Mexico, parts of the 11th Cavalry rode at least 1,000 miles. On April 12th, less than a month after crossing the border, part of the 13th Cavalry rode into Parral, Chihuahua, 400 miles south of Columbus. If the bitter action in Columbus turned out to be an eye-opener for Pancho Villa, those flying columns of the Punitive Expedition proved no less so. Small, hard-riding columns of gringo troopers crisscrossed Chihuahua, surprising groups of Villistas, riding them into the ground. Pancho Villa, the original desert fox, found some worthy hunters on his tail.

(It should be noted that Villa was also trying to elude groups of Mexican federal troops during this same period. Chihuahua was Villa's backyard, where he could count on help from many locals, but it's certainly to his credit that he was not captured by either the U.S. troopers or the Carranzistas during this undoubtedly dangerous time. It is said, however, that he was wounded at Guerrero in a brush with Carranzistas and may have been holed up someplace, recovering from the wound, during most of the time the U.S. cavalrymen were galloping around in Chihuahua trying to find him and his men.)

These U.S. Cavalry troopers are driving some Mexicans back across the Rio Grande. **Rio Grande Historical Collections, New Mexico State University Library**

The separate columns of U.S. Cavalry proved to be guerrilla raiders in their own right, covering a lot of ground and hitting with surprise and dash. Discipline and superior musketry weighed heavily on the side of the gringos during any engagements. They marched over snow-filled mountain passes and across hot deserts. The men cooked their own food (what little there was of it) in their mess kits over open fires. At night the mounts shivered on the picket lines, the men, curled up on the ground, shivered in their blankets. Men and horses grew lean. (One troop commander commented after the expedition that it would be a good idea to fit saddles to horses when they are thin rather than when they are fat after months of garrison duty.) The men's ragged uniforms flapped in the constant wind. Lips cracked and bled; red eyes stared across the empty land. Casualties were light, but a few cavalry boys remained behind in Mexico, buried wrapped in their blankets. Career soldiers who had been in the service so long that they could remember the campaigns of the Indian Wars recalled the Punitive Expedition as their toughest campaign: wind, heat, snow, bullets, and empty bellies. In a hostile country. The Mexicans of whatever faction resented the gringo intrusion into their country and what they considered their affairs.

Besides minor brushes with Villistas and Carranzistas, the cavalrymen fought large engagements (up to a few hundred men on each side) at Parral, Guerrero, Aguas Calientes, Ojos Azules, and Carrizal during March, April, May, and June of 1916. At Guerrero, about 400 men of the 7th Cavalry surprised a larger force of Villistas, killing many, dispersing the rest. At Parral, a couple of troops of the 13th Cavalry had to fight their way loose from an apparent trap by Carranzistas. The 10th Cavalry easily dispersed a group of Villistas at Aguas Calientes. At Ojos Azules the 11th Cavalry, with their Apache scouts from the United States, routed another band of Villistas.

So there they were, thousands of American soldiers scattered all over Chihuahua, their food and ammo running short, their horses just about played out. Small detachments of cavalrymen chasing around hundreds of miles south of the border. A possible disaster was in the making should the Mexican federal troops decide to try to destroy one of the small columns. They needed supplies.

The U.S. Army had assumed it would commandeer the Mexican railways in order to move supplies into Chihuahua. The Mexican government said no. If Pancho Villa was a pain in the neck, he was *their* pain in the neck, and they preferred the gringo soldiers just turn around and head north. And the U.S. State Department, trying to avoid a real war with the Mexicans, told the Army boys to lay off. Don't touch the railroads was the word that came down the lines from Washington.

The cavalry columns were so deep in Mexico and so widely dispersed that packtrains, or horse- or mule-drawn escort wagons did not have the capacity or range to supply them. How to get supplies into Mexico?

Onto the scene charged Major General Hugh L. Scott, Chief of Staff, a tough and feisty old soldier whose career would eventually span the Indian Wars out on the plains to World War I in France. Appalled and angered by what he considered gross lack of concern over at the State Department for the welfare of American soldiers, Scott telephoned the Quartermaster General and asked how much it would cost to buy enough motor vehicles to supply the troops. Just about $450,000 came the quick reply. Buy them, Scott ordered, realizing full

A motley group of U.S. soldiers with an equally motley collection of weapons, in front of one of the adobe huts they built for their stay in Namiquipa, Chihuahua. The rifles were probably captured from the Mexicans. **Columbus Historical Society**

Infantrymen marching through a Mexican pueblo after the 1916 raid.

well that only Congress can approve such an expenditure.

The Army had a few automobiles and trucks already, but they were scattered at posts all over the States. In any event, there weren't enough of them to offset the lack of use of the Mexican railroads the soldiers had counted on. A few vehicles had been tested during the maneuvers of 1911, but the Army had very few drivers and mechanics. The U.S. Army was still a nineteenth century army when it rode away on horseback to chase Villa across Chihuahua; it moved by foot and was pulled by horses and mules. But times were a-changing. Fast.

Secretary of War Baker, although new to his job, had enough gumption to stand behind the old soldier so he wouldn't have to end his career behind bars. With one phone call, General Scott moved the U.S. Army emphatically into the Motor Age and the twentieth century.

Suddenly the Army owned as motley a collection of motorized rolling stock as it has owned since. Legend has it that vehicles intended for the war in France, for the British and French armies, were pulled right off the dock in New York. Manufacturers entrained vehicles along with drivers and mechanics and headed them toward Columbus. Scott had the foresight to hire civilian drivers, realizing that few soldiers knew how to drive. Almost six hundred trucks and over seventy automobiles were purchased and sent to the border.

Trucks: Peerless, Velie, Locomobile, Packard, Mack, White, Jeffrey "Quads" (4x4s!), and many others; tankers, wreckers, cargo trucks, machine shop trucks. Automobiles: Dodges, Fords, Chevrolets, Studebakers, Buicks, Oaklands. Most of the automobiles were Dodge touring cars, the car that is now associated with the Punitive Expedition. The Dodge tourer for 1916 weighed 2,250 pounds and developed 35 h.p. in a 212.3 c.i., four-cylinder L-head engine. This stock tourer was probably the first motor vehicle owned by the U.S. Army to go into "battle." Some of these vehicles later saw service in France. One of them, found in France many years after WWI, was shipped to West Point and restored by the cadets; it can be seen at the museum there.

Although hindered by political niceties (the American military would have to get used to that), the Army was able to solve its basic supply problem with motor trucks. It's very possible that the Punitive Expedition could not have succeeded without them. Two truck companies were formed at Fort Bliss. Until those two truck companies set out for Columbus from Fort Bliss, no military convoys consisting of so many motor vehicles had ever been tried over such a long distance. The trip was a revelation to the officers in charge. The companies were made up of Whites and Jeffrey Quads, with drivers and mechanics sent along from the factories. Many of the civilian drivers who later went south of the border were armed and subject to military discipline.

A few White trucks and an Indian motorcycle in Columbus. **Columbus Historical Society**

However, they proved difficult to discipline, most of them could not stand the rugged duty on campaign, and their high pay ($100 a month) was resented by the soldiers (privates earned only $21 a month). The civilian drivers were replaced as fast as talented soldiers could be trained. One aging sergeant had his heart so set on learning to drive that he even sent off for a correspondence course; he failed in the face of the real thing, an apparent case of too old a dog trying to learn too new a trick.

Trucks started rolling down the trail to Colonia Dublan, Chihuahua, the day after they arrived in Columbus. These first convoys were not well organized. Equip-

ment and supplies "disappeared." Trucks broke down and goods were "salvaged" from them. Soon enough, however, the Quartermaster Corps developed a system that allowed them to get most of their trucks and supplies where they belonged without losing so much along the road.

Eventually seventy-four truck companies were organized. Equipment kept arriving almost every day by train to be unloaded along the railway sidings: trucks, truck bodies, spare parts. As far as most of the soldiers in Columbus were concerned they may as well have been faced with a collection of harpsichords to assemble; all of the mechanical contraptions meant damned

Ambulances lined up in Columbus, New Mexico, during the Punitive Expedition. These are White vehicles. **Museum of New Mexico**

International relations. A grimy truck driver in coveralls poses with a handsome Mexican woman.
Columbus Historical Society

This is a Jeffrey Quad, a 4x4 truck used to great advantage in Mexico. The radiator guards could be dismounted for use as cooking grills. Note the rifle boot in front of the driver's position.
Columbus Historical Society

little to men who were accustomed to issuing saddles and bridles. Somehow, all of that complicated junk had to be put together.

The First Aero Squadron saved the day. Luckily for the Quartermaster Corps, the First Aero Squadron, with all of its "aeroplanes" (eight Curtiss Jennys) and almost all of the mechanics in the Army, had received its orders on March 12th to join the expedition. When the airplane mechanics and riggers weren't busy with their Jennys, they pitched in and bolted bodies to trucks and got the trucks rolling south. The Aero Squadron mechanics also set up a machine shop. General Pershing had always been interested in new developments. It was his idea to bring the airplanes into the expedition, thinking they might come in handy scouting out the Villistas. Although the squadron's pilots had little luck finding Pancho Villa and his boys, it proved to be a lucky thing the airplane mechanics were on hand in Columbus.

The truck convoys started rolling south. Slowly. A trip of a few hundred miles into Mexico and return could take weeks. Twenty to thirty trucks made up a truck train, and with experience came the realization that all the trucks in one train should be, as far as practicable, of the same make in order to facilitate repairs. Operating in hostile country, a truck's crew could not be left behind to guard it. And if a truck had to be left alone, its load would probably be stolen by passing soldiers and the vehicle stripped by passing truck trains. If one truck wheezed or thumped to a halt, the entire column stopped while repairs were made, if repairs could be made. If not, the load was distributed, useful parts were taken from the vehicle, and it was abandoned. Skeletonized motor vehicles became common along the roads in Chihuahua, although not as

A loaded truck train heads off into Mexico.
Columbus Historical Society

Truck Co. No. 2 drove White trucks, which may have been the most versatile vehicles used in Mexico.
Columbus Historical Society

common as the skeletons of the draft animals they were meant to replace. During the entire time the Punitive Expedition was in Mexico, the pack trains and trains of animal-drawn escort wagons continued to pound the trails into Mexico; the motor trucks were never enough to carry the entire load of supplies needed by the troops.

Every conceivable military load was trucked off into Mexico, as well as candy, chewing gum, and tobacco. The boys south of the border would not be denied their comforts. After a time, as the numbers of troops in Mexico increased (to a maximum of about 10,000), a limit of two trucks per train was established for carrying mail and luxuries. The American soldier, like his brothers before and after, yearned for news from home. Limping infantrymen might be picked up on return trips, men going on leave. Damaged equipment was carried north for repairs. One memorable load included all the sabers of one of the cavalry units. The horse soldiers had discovered that the Mexicans, like the Plains Indians, would not hold still for a saber charge. To the dismay of young George Patton, who had designed it, the cavalrymen considered the saber just a clanking impediment, useless in guerrilla warfare.

If anything, the roads south of the border were worse than those in the States. The roads indicated on the maps were not roads as most gringo drivers understood such things, but just wandering wagon trails across the country. When the trails became muddy during the summer rains, the trucks would spread out, looking for solid ground, until the "road" might be a half mile wide in the flat regions. The road wound steeply in and out of canyons, crossed arroyos and streams, and was full of rocks and holes. That the trucks held together as well as they did was a credit to the manufacturers. Certainly the designers of the vehicles had never envisioned such abuse for them. These were primitive machines in a primitive land. Gas lines broke, carbs choked up with dust, springs broke under full loads, even solid steel

wheels collapsed. The engineers worked at the road, trying to improve it, but there was too much road, too little equipment, and too little time to do much except try to make it at least passable. The worst was the mud, and at times the trains had to be halted in their tracks until the ground could dry out.

The trail followed by the truckers, after preliminary problems were ironed out, went to Colonia Dublan, then to Galeana, El Valle, Las Cruces, and Namiquipa. For the most part, trucking operations did not go beyond Namiquipa, which lay less than two hundred miles south of Columbus. In spite of the apparently short distance, a round trip could take two weeks.

The commander of the truck train rode out in front or in the rear in his Dodge touring car, his driver straddling the ruts because of the relatively low clearance of the automobile as compared to the trucks. The first truck in the column was usually the kitchen truck, and a cooker was devised out of milk cans so that hot coffee could be served at lunch stops or when the column stopped for a break or repairs. Supper and breakfast were cooked over pits, and the radiator guard of one of the trucks would be dismounted and laid over the wood fire to serve as a cooking grill. If a truck train counted twenty to thirty trucks, then the personnel in one of the trains could run as high as eighty-five men, counting two drivers for each truck, the commander and his driver, a couple of mechanics, and the guards.

Each train carried a squad of infantry who "rode shotgun." A few of them might be perched on top of the loads, scanning the country around, scaring off any large number of Mexicans they might see by putting a few warning rifle shots in their direction. The guards were ordered not to fire unless they were attacked, but the men and officers in the individual truck trains might interpret what constituted an impending danger rather liberally. Some of the squad would ride in the kitchen truck in front, the rest in the truck at the rear of

A bunch of the boys whooping it up in a Dodge tourer. The ubiquitous Dodge tourer became the symbol of the motor vehicles in Mexico.
Columbus Historical Society

The vehicle appears to be a Buick. According to some scribbling on the back of the photo, the driver's name is Wells.
Columbus Historical Society

the column. Legend has it that the infantrymen became proficient at shooting craps in the bouncing, rolling trucks. Anything to relieve the boredom. At night they served as sentinels, because the drivers and mechanics had work to do repairing the trucks or they were too tired to do anything but roll up their blankets under the trucks to get as much rest as they could before another day of wrestling the awkward machines through the boondocks. The trucks were "circled" at night if bandit activity was reported in the area, but no attack was ever mounted against one of the large truck trains.

At night, by the light of kerosene lanterns, the two mechanics who were situated (ideally) with each train would make what repairs they could. Each train carried some spare parts. And each truck carried a ten gallon milk can full of water so the truck trains did not have to depend on water holes, which could be, at certain times of the year, undependable, and were (one could easily imagine if one happened to be worried about such things) dandy places to set up an ambush. After a while, as the individual truck train commanders gained experience, they found it preferable to camp where night found them; they were carrying water and wood, and by camping alone away from the rest of the army they could control how they wanted to live.

On the return trip to Columbus, the trucks were run through the machine shop and inspected and repaired. Then, after the crews had a brief rest and a bath, they might load up and head right back down the trail. As things turned out, the motor truck became an almost indispensable part of the Punitive Expedition.

* * *

AND THE MOTOR CARS. With his command scattered to hell and gone across Chihuahua, Black Jack Pershing decided the only way he could exercise control and get a

A truck train in Mexico. These are Whites, which were the trucks used in 20 of the truck companies. If a manufacturer wanted to sell trucks to the government, he had to prove them on the firing line . . . in Mexico.   **Museum of New Mexico**

feel for the campaign was to get right into the thick of it, and he did so by mounting up in a car and catching up with the cavalry command wherever he could. Legend tells us that he went on the trail after Villa in a Dodge, but extant photos show him next to what looks like a Buick.

Pershing took his headquarters on the road, and from March until the end of May he was at the "front," trying to get a handle on developments, sleeping on the ground next to his car, his "office" in a box he carried in the car. Three or four cars made up the headquarters column when it was on the road, and with him he had a couple of aides, a stenographer, drivers, a cook, and several infantrymen who acted as bodyguards. Often, too, a car full of correspondents tagged along behind. It is interesting to note that the commander of the Punitive Expedition would go riding off into the blue, across hostile country, with just a few men, ignoring the obvious danger. A tough, intelligent, enterprising man, but it is also said of him that he may have been trying to put some distance between himself and personal tragedy; his wife and daughters had died in a fire just the year before.

General Pershing's closest call on these wild excursions came near the end of April. Trekking across un-

mapped terrain one day, the party was still on the road when night caught them. As they ground slowly along, an armed Mexican appeared in the trail in front of them. George Patton was in the lead car. Getting down to talk to the Mexican, he spotted many more armed men in the brush around them. Pershing's car pulled up alongside Patton's, and the third machine came to a stop on the other side of Pershing's car, thereby affording the general some protection.

Lieutenant Patton, who could speak Spanish, went forward to see if the Mexicans were "friendly." He was explaining to the Mexicans that they were the advance guard of a motorized regiment when Pershing appeared beside him. The general announced, "loud and clear," that he was General Pershing and he demanded to know by what right the Mexicans would dare to halt the American cars. The Mexicans, apparently stunned by Pershing's commanding presence, let the three cars continue unmolested. That the Americans were in real danger was proved to everybody's satisfaction when three trucks loaded with airplane spare parts and fuel were attacked in almost that same place, apparently by the same group of Mexicans. None of the Americans in the truck convoy was injured, although many shots were exchanged.

Artillery being transported by truck on the border. What the U.S. Army learned about transport during the border crisis would be of great use when the boys got to France.   **Rio Grande Historical Collections, New Mexico State University Library**

It might be interesting to pause and reflect for a minute on the few casualties suffered by the American troops during the Punitive Expedition. The Villistas, for the most part, were villagers, sometimes Indians, poor people who knew little of mechanical things. Recent studies have indicated that people who have shared in the Industrial Revolution also make better soldiers when it comes to handling modern weapons. They understand the connection between laying the sights of their weapons on the target and the laying of bullets in the same place. "Primitive" people are more difficult to teach in this respect.

To compound their problem, the Villistas used a variety of weapons: Winchesters and Remingtons (sporting weapons, really), Mausers captured from federal troops, and old Krags. Many of these weapons were rusty old clunkers that had been through years of revolution. The Mexicans had little ammunition to waste on target practice, but, once engaged, Villistas managed to make plenty of noise. They weren't afraid to fight, and this in itself could be intimidating to a force of reluctant federal conscripts. But against truly disciplined troops, men who prized marksmanship and horsemanship, the Villistas stood little chance in a more or less evenly matched fire fight. The men of the U.S. Cavalry were such troops.

* * *

IN HIS LETTERS HOME, Colonel Charles S. Farnsworth, 16th Infantry, has left us a record of motoring experiences with the Punitive Expedition. In his car they would carry a couple pieces of canvas with ropes tied to them. When stuck in sand, they would jack up the car and lay the canvas under the tires; then, once rolling, they would pull the canvas back into the car with the attached ropes so they wouldn't have to stop. Burned-out clutches were a common problem. Very often they would have to travel for miles in first or second gear because of the rough roads. If they had to travel through long stretches of sand while climbing a grade, they would drain the water and refill the radiator with cooler water, trying to keep the machinery at a reasonable temperature. They carried a ten gallon "desert bag" and a few canteens full of water, and they always had chains stored in case they ran into mud.

Colonel Farnsworth learned never to trust the locals to point out a good spot to ford a stream; by bitter experience, he learned they were not beyond helping a motorist get stuck so they could assist in pulling him out—for a price, of course. As the truck trains became common, he passed four in one day. There was no doubt about it, the U.S. Army had entered the Motor Age.

* * *

AND IT TOOK the motor car into battle. It seems fitting that the U.S. Army's foremost exponent and practitioner of mechanized warfare should have been the first one to ride a motor car to a fight. On May 14th, 1916, Lt. George S. Patton, while on a corn-buying expedition, learned that one of Villa's henchmen was holed up at a nearby ranch. Patton had fourteen men with him and they were mounted in that most unlikely chariot of war—the ubiquitous Dodge tourer. Their prey, Julio Cardenas, was reportedly at a hacienda just north of Rubio.

Patton was in the first car. Just as they topped a rise leading to the ranch, Patton told the driver to open her up. As they raced past the house, Patton saw one of a group of men who was skinning a cow jump up and run into the house, as if in a hurry to warn somebody of their presence. The car skidded to a quick stop just past the corner of the ranch house and Patton jumped out with his Springfield in his hand. He was also armed with a pistol. One of his men followed behind him. The other two Dodges stopped just short of the ranch house. Six men dismounted from those two cars and charged the other side of the structure.

The ranch house was of a traditional Spanish colonial design with an enclosed courtyard. Just as Patton hurried toward the main gate, three horsemen galloped out of it. Patton drew his pistol and ordered them to halt. He was not sure who they were, and as standing orders

Two Indian motorcycles on the border at the time of Pancho Villa's incursion. The machine gun is a Lewis gun. **Rio Grande Historical Collections, New Mexico State University Library**

Another view of an Indian motorcycle mounting a machine gun. As it turned out, a motorcycle proved to be too bumpy a perch for a machine gun. **Rio Grande Historical Collections, New Mexico State University Library**

prohibited any firing except defensively, Patton did not dare be overly trigger-happy. He was a good soldier.

But the three mounted Mexicans turned and rode away from Patton—until the other six men of the assault party came around the corner of the ranch house. The Mexicans then pulled up their horses, turned again, and galloped back at Patton, shooting as they came. Bullets threw up pebbles in front of Patton and the man with him. Patton fired five times with his pistol, the range about twenty yards. Just then the men at the other end of the house started firing, so Patton and the other American ducked around the corner as bullets smacked into the adobe wall and powdered them with dust. Two of Patton's shots had gone home, breaking the arm of one of the Mexicans and putting a bullet in his horse's belly.

Hearing the shooting, the other men from Patton's car ran up to assist. Patton looked around the corner and saw another man on a horse right in front of him. Another shot from Patton's pistol (he had quickly reloaded) and that horse went down with a broken hip. As the Mexican disentangled himself from his mount and rose, Patton and the men with him all fired at the same time, killing the man. Just then they spotted another armed Mexican about a hundred yards away. Patton fired three quick shots at him with his Springfield, while the others fired at the same time, and they put that man out of action.

Another Mexican showed up, running along the wall to the south of them. Patton watched one of his men fire, shake his head in disappointment, fire again and grin as the bandit fell. This was the rider Patton had originally wounded in the arm. He had ridden his horse back into the courtyard, run into the house and jumped out one of the windows, and was trying to get away on foot when Patton's grinning marksman nailed him with a .30-'06 round. Still, the Mexican was only wounded. As another American went up to him, the Mexican raised his one good arm as if to surrender, then grabbed his pistol and fired, missing. The American put a round through the man's head, ending the fight for the Mexican once and for all.

Then, as Cardenas was reported to have a band of about thirty-five men with him, Patton climbed onto the roof of the house to see if more bandits were inside. He was afraid the Mexicans, if there proved to be a large band of them, would themselves gain the advantage of the roof and fire down on the Americans. However, a natural booby trap awaited the young lieutenant. The roofs of Mexican houses in Chihuahua at that time were (still are, although to a lesser extent) built with just the materials at hand. They put *vigas*, round beams, from wall to wall, then lay small branches, *latillas*, across the beams, and then cover the whole with six inches or so of earth. Such a construction can serve quite well as a roof, and provides wonderful natural insulation, but can, if not properly maintained, erode. Patton went through the roof to his armpits. It's a good thing no Villistas were hiding in the room below!

Extricating himself (and one can imagine rather quickly), Patton surveyed the courtyard and found it empty. Afraid to jump inside alone, he judiciously went back down the way he had climbed up. The man who would become famous and feared for his audacious tank attacks managed to keep his wits about him. He called over the group of Mexicans who had been skinning the cow. They had not joined in the fight, nor had the American soldiers fired at them. Using the Mexican cow skinners as a shield, the small force of Americans entered the ranch house for a search. Inside the rooms

A White truck has slipped into the ditch in spite of having chains mounted on the rear double wheels.
Columbus Historical Society

An army touring car hesitates before attempting a flooded road. The Punitive Expedition operated during the summer rainy season.
Columbus Historical Society

they found only old men, women, and the woman and baby of Julio Cardenas.

It was then that they learned they had killed Cardenas, who was the first man Patton had shot, the man who refused to give up until his brains were blown out. The two others were also Villistas, Isador Lopez and Juan Garza. The American soldiers tied the dead Mexicans across the car hoods and pulled out just as a troop of about forty Villistas galloped onto the scene. The Americans did not stay around to discover the reaction of these Mexicans to the gory trophies they now had strapped across the cars. Passing through Rubio, it was observed that the local citizens got a bit agitated at the sight of Cardenas and his comrades dripping blood down the louvered hoods of the gringo cars. Patton and the boys made it back to camp without further incident, and as a reward for his efforts, Patton was allowed to keep Cardenas' silver-mounted saddle and saber.

Most histories of Patton, if they mention the incident at the ranch at all, tell us that the young lieutenant shot the three Mexicans out of the saddle. Not quite, but it seems he was handy enough with his sidearms to indicate that the pearl-handled revolvers he sported during World War II were not just macho ornaments.

After a couple months of the "active pursuit" period of the Punitive Expedition, the Army was pulled back to Colonia Dublan and other posts in the northern part of Chihuahua. By that time Pancho Villa's men were scat-

tered all over—those who hadn't been killed in battle with the U.S. Cavalry or the Carranzista troops. If Villa was hurting before he hit Columbus, two months of playing hare and hound with U.S. horse soldiers almost finished him. He never again menaced the border.

With the troops pulled back into the north—the State Department was worred about the active pursuit—they were easier to supply. The Cavalry did run scouting patrols, but their orders were to steer clear of any engagements, especially any trouble with federal troops, most of whom resented the gringo invasion as much as Pancho Villa and the other citizens of Chihuahua. With trouble impending with Germany, the Wilson government did its best to avoid an out-and-out war with the Mexicans. We came very close to this, however, over an incident at Carrizal, on June 21st, 1916.

The men of Troops C and K of the 10th Cavalry—the legendary black "Buffalo Soldiers," Pershing's old regiment—were on a scouting mission when they came to Carrizal, a town full of Mexican Carranzista troops, armed with machine guns and led by determined officers. The commander of the American troops had been told personally, by Pershing, to avoid trouble, to go around trouble, to run away from it as long as his column was not being shot at.

The American, Captain Boyd, insisted on riding through Carrizal. The Mexicans were just as insistent that he would not. Boyd could have ridden around the

A meeting of the old and the new. A truck train pauses by a train of escort wagons. Below, truck drivers with an escort wagon. Other escort wagons can be seen in the background; the motor vehicles were not able to carry everything the troops needed. **Columbus Historical Society**

The White Company made at least 70 of these vehicles. The units could set up in 12 minutes and send messages within a radius of 800 miles. The machines were equipped with a power transmission for driving the electrical generator. The motorcycle is an Indian, no doubt used for carrying messages. **Fort Bliss Museum**

place. He was outnumbered four to one. The Mexicans had the advantage of cover in the town. Exactly what went through Boyd's mind will never be known. In any event, Troops C and K dismounted and made an assault. They were badly cut up. They took cover and returned the fire, killing and wounding many Mexicans. They killed the Mexican general in charge of the detachment, but they couldn't dislodge the Mexicans and they had to retire. They left behind thirteen dead, ten wounded, and twenty-four captured. The American prisoners were quickly returned to El Paso by the Mexican government.

This was the only defeat suffered by American troops during the Punitive Expedition. It was fought with the wrong people under impossible conditions. Captain Boyd was killed there at Carrizal, and it's probably lucky for him he was; the unfortunate affair caused Pershing a lot of embarrassment and anguish for the men killed and wounded; generals do not enjoy unnecessary casualties and having to try to rationalize the

An early armored car used on the border. **Fort Bliss Museum**

stupidity and arrogance of their officers.

Carrizal was the last heavy fighting of the Punitive Expedition, although the troops stayed in Mexico until February of 1917. After Carrizal, and until they left Mexico for France, the boys had to fight that more common enemy of soldiers: boredom. They lived in the dusty camps, ate sand with their meals, and watched for Villa, whom they never found.

Much derision has been expended in the direction of Pershing and his cavalrymen because they did not capture Villa. In fact, their orders were to simply find his men, kill or capture them, disperse his bands so they would not be an effective fighting force. The original orders had read "capture Villa," but General Scott, with a bit more wisdom, suggested that sending thousands of men to catch one man was a pretty silly notion. What if Villa goes to Argentina? Are we to send our men down there? No. The orders were amended. On the other hand, it seems unlikely that any cavalry officer in

Mexico wouldn't have traded his string of polo ponies to get his hands on Villa. But the cavalrymen were ordered to pull back. The reins were applied from Washington. Pershing and his officers would have known just how their descendents in Korea and Viet Nam felt many years later.

From March of 1916 until February of 1917 the truck trains rolled up and down the trails out of Columbus. Thousands of tons of supplies were carried into Mexico. General Scott's vision and daring, to say nothing for his disdain of bureaucracy in time of an emergency, had paid off. Hundreds of successful trips were made as the U.S. Army learned a new trade.

E.A. Capen, asked what he thought of the newfangled motor transport he observed on the border when he was a young man, chuckled and said: "It worked okay when it worked."

It worked just often enough.

This Dodge touring car is on display at the museum at West Point. Found in France many years after the war, it was returned to the United States and restored by some of the cadets. It may have served on the border, but there is no proof of this. **West Point Museum**

Coast to Coast
with the Doughboys

The First Transcontinental Military Convoy
(Photos by Lt. Col. Dwight Eisenhower)

O N THE AFTERNOON of the 13th of July, 1919, Harvey Firestone threw a garden party at his home in Columbiana, Ohio, for almost three hundred soldiers: officers and men of Companies E and F of the 433rd Motor Supply Train, Service Unit #595, Company E of the 5th Engineers, a medical detachment, a field artillery detachment, and about seventeen staff officers. The men were resting for the day during the first crossing of the continent by a U.S. Army motor convoy. Among the staff officers, who had been sent along by the War Department as observers, was a twenty-nine-year-old lieutenant colonel from the Tank Corps by the name of Dwight D. Eisenhower.

A five-minute movie of the event at the Firestone place is on file at the Eisenhower Library in Abilene, Kansas. The film starts at the men's camp, showing them getting ready for the party while local citizens wander around gawking. In spite of the recent war, the convoy was the first time for most Americans to see so many soldiers in one place. Motorcycles and Dodge tourers snort around in the camp, laying down trails of exhaust smoke. Later, at Firestone's home, Harvey Firestone himself chats animatedly with Lt. Col. Charles W. McClure, the tall Expedition Commander.

The men ate under canvas and were attended by servants. Then they emerged into the sunlight, lighting up their smokes, hitching up britches and pulling on campaign hats, grimacing and clowning self-conciously at the camera. Mutt and Jeff, the tallest and shortest men in the convoy, stroll by arm in arm. Time for high jinks, men stand on their heads in the grass and roll tires around with men curled up inside. Possibly they should have saved their energy, but few of them were entirely aware of what awaited them west of the Mississippi . . .

This first transcontinental military motor trip was the idea of Captain Bernard H. McMahon, who did most of the planning for the trip and went along as Train Commander. The U.S. Army had purchased many motor vehicles during the war, but the war had not lasted long enough for them to be tested on active service in France; all of the special-purpose vehicles would get a chance to show their stuff on the road to the Golden Gate. On the way, the men would stage a military maneuver of sorts; that is, they would demonstrate the practicability of moving an armed force across the country in motor vehicles, having assumed that railroad bridges

Somewhere west of Cheyenne, two officers stand tall in a stiff breeze. The 29-year-old lieutenant colonel on the left is Dwight Eisenhower; the other man, Major Sereno Brett. The two men were in the Tank Corps and the War Department had assigned them as observers to accompany the first transcontinental military convoy. The convoy left Washington, D.C., on July 7, 1919, and arrived in San Francisco on the 6th of September 1919. **Dwight D. Eisenhower Library**

Coast to Coast with the Doughboys

The transcontinental military convoy would test many vehicles procured by the Army during WWI but never used in active service. The vehicles on the long march included Cadillac and Dodge touring cars, White reconnaissance cars, Standard "B" trucks, a Cadillac truck carrying a searchlight, Dodge, F.W.D., Garford, G.M.C., Mack, Packard, Riker, and White trucks, Harley-Davidson and Indian motorcycles, and two tractors. Over 80 vehicles were in the convoy, but some civilian autos were donated by the manufacturers to be tested on the cross-country run and these do not appear on any official list of convoy equipment.
Dwight D. Eisenhower Library

and tunnels had been damaged or destroyed by agents of an Asiatic enemy (guess who). As they rolled west, the troops would have to overcome all natural and mechanical problems by themselves.

It was thought, too, that folks all across the country would surely enjoy seeing at least a small part of the military machine they had put together during the war, and it was hoped that several hundred of the small town and farm boys who would see the expedition would become excited enough to join up. Demobilization had gone so fast that the Army needed some recruits. Another reason for the trip, and not the least of them, was to show America the actual condition of her "highways." The 1919 military trek was a road test, a war game, a parade, a recruiting expedition, all rolled into one, bouncing across the country at an average speed of 6.07 mph, 58.1 miles per day.

As far as Tanker Dwight Eisenhower was concerned, the trip might prove an escape. His requests to accompany the Punitive Expedition of 1916 to Mexico had been turned down. Then, during the World War, his applications for service in France had been rejected while he trained other men to go. He made so many applications for active service that he was reprimanded. At last he was ready to be shipped over on November 18th, 1918 as commander of a tank outfit. But the Armistice went into effect on the 11th of November.

The end of what everybody knew would be the last war in history found Ike waiting on the dock, possibly the most frustrated soldier in America. He shuddered at the thought of trying to explain to his son "what Daddy did in the War," and he cringed at the notion of having to attend reunions with the other members of the West Point class of 1915, most of whom had seen

Coast to Coast with the Doughboys

service in France. Even if Ike could have foreseen that his duties during WWI would be precisely the training he would need for his job in the next war, it is doubtful that would have been of much consolation to him in 1919. He had missed the Great Adventure.

Ike didn't even have the comfort of a home life; quarters for married officers were scarce at Camp Meade where he was helping with the tedious work of demobilizing the wartime army, so Mamie and their son had to remain at her family home in Denver. When Ike heard that the War Department wanted two officers of the Tank Corps to accompany the cross-country convoy as observers, he and his Tank Corps buddy, Major Sereno Brett, were the first in line. They joined the truck convoy at Frederick, Maryland, its first stop, just forty-six miles out of Washington, D.C.

When Ike and Brett showed up at the fairgrounds at Frederick, they met some discouraged troopers. Lack of progress. Repairs even on that first day. Lack of control in the column.

Most of the observers agreed the convoy had been thrown together too hastily. Too many of the trucks suffered from breakdowns caused by a need for minor adjustments that might have been discovered if the vehicles had been given at least a brief testing period before they were loaded up and pointed down the trail to California. Some of the "drivers," it was discovered, must have had more experience behind mules than behind the wheel of a motor vehicle. Legend has it that a few were heard to shout "Whoa!" as their machines plunged out of control into ditches. One neophyte learned something about shifting gears when he put his transmission into reverse while going downhill.

Many of the men of the 433rd Motor Supply Train were the rawest of recruits, men without any notion of military discipline or military courtesy, on a first name basis with everybody, no matter what their rank, or who they were. The Regular Army types and the West Pointers were, to say the least, distressed. Those among them who knew what lay ahead gave little hope that

The military convoy set out to see if it could cross the U.S. on its own, assuming that railroad bridges and tunnels had been damaged or destroyed by an Asiatic enemy. The trip was a military maneuver. The men maintained their schedule until they got to Nebraska, where the roads started to deteriorate.

Dwight D. Eisenhower Library

Coast to Coast with the Doughboys

Almost 300 men accompanied the convoy. Many of them were the rawest of recruits when they started out, and many "drivers" had but the vaguest notion of how to operate the vehicles. They learned the hard way, although their lessons were hard on the machinery. It was noted by military observers that by the time they got to California they were all good drivers. Small wonder, considering the primitive roads they had to cover.
Dwight D. Eisenhower Library

the ragtag outfit would ever reach San Francisco. They were damn near right.

Every vehicle was inspected by three officers before it started the day's march. The longest day's run was ninety miles, the shortest four. The machines were filled with water, oil and gasoline at the end of the day. They were cleaned, if possible, and adjustments and repairs were made in the evening. The mechanics of Service Unit #595, commanded by 2nd Lt. G.N. Bissell, turned in superb work. The daily litany of broken fan belts, blown head gaskets, burned bearings, fouled spark plugs, burned out magnetos is too long and tedious to repeat here.

To give credit where credit is due, however, it was noted that Edward A. Reis, a civilian employee of the Ordnance Department, was a "mature mechanic" without whose skill many of the trucks never would have reached California. Mr. Reis was along on the trip solely to accompany the five-ton artillery tractor, the Militor, but—a good sport—he pitched in wherever he was needed.

It was conceded, too, that the trip could not have succeeded without the Militor wheeled

tractor and the small caterpillar-type tractor. The small tractor was carried on one of the heavy cargo trucks, but the Militor brought up the rear of the column, dragging vehicles out of ditches, towing trucks that had broken down. The Militor could tow several vehicles at once, so it might show up at camp in the evening with four or five trucks and cars jerking along behind it. Both tractors were used extensively pulling trucks through mud, sand and streams, and up steep hills, and almost any hill proved to be "steep" for most of the large trucks.

Two motorcyclists would leave camp a half hour early each morning. They were Captain Arthur Harrington and 1st Lt. Ralph Enos, two aviators who had been assigned to the convoy as observers. They would go biking off into the unknown with *The Complete Official Road Guide of the Lincoln Highway* and a collection of salmon-colored isosceles triangles. Using their road guide and directions from locals, the boys would tack up their triangles on fence posts, telegraph poles, barns, trees. The angle at which they tacked them up would mean straight ahead, right turn, or left turn. Harrington and Enos

Coast to Coast with the Doughboys

must have been good trailblazers; getting lost seems to be about the only problem not encountered by this first transcontinental military convoy.

Bridges: Too small, some of them covered with roofs too low for the taller trucks, too flimsy, nonexistent. The engineers rebuilt bridges, built new bridges, helped pull trucks out of scary situations when they crashed through bridges. Weather: 50 mph winds in Wyoming, below freezing in the Rockies, 110 degrees Fahrenheit in Nevada. Heavy rains would dissolve roads. Roads: Of the 3,251 miles traveled by the expedition, 1,778 miles were on dirt roads, mud, sand, mountain paths, wagon trails, and in one place an abandoned railroad line.

The convoy diary records all of the woes the first cross-country motorists would have encountered, compounded by the fact—so they discovered—that many of the vehicles, especially the large cargo trucks, were too heavy and clumsy for wilderness trekking. Trucks could sink several feet into mud or quicksand, necessitating massive excavations to extricate them. Fatigue: The convoy was on a prearranged schedule. It had been planned that every Sunday should be a rest period, but much of the time they had to push seven days a week. Men who had been on the Western Front suggested that for a war game the transcontinental convoy came close to the real thing, as far as work was concerned.

But the trek wasn't all work. The convoy passed through some 350 communities and about 3,250,000 Americans saw it. Hearing of the approach of the column, folks would go into town to wave flags and serve the passing doughboys coffee, lemonade, and sandwiches. According to the military observers, a few people seemed disappointed by the convoy; but most citizens

The military convoy passed through about 350 communities and it was estimated that 3,250,000 people got a chance to see it. Local citizens would make sandwiches and coffee and lemonade for the men. Picnics, dinners, and dances were held for them, although the men paid for the hospitality by having to listen to many patriotic speeches.
Dwight D. Eisenhower Library

Coast to Coast with the Doughboys

showed the boys a grand time, even organizing street dances and picnics. The men had to suffer through more patriotic speeches than they cared to listen to, but local hospitality gave them a chance to ogle the native "prairie chickens."

For Dwight Eisenhower the convoy turned out to be something of a lark, a chance to release pent-up energy. Camping out with officers from back east gave Ike and Major Brett a devilish inspiration. At one remote town, Brett convinced the denizens of a restaurant to talk loud and hard about the "Indian troubles" they were supposedly experiencing. The eastern officers, hearing the conversations, took the bait, and later that night when they heard "Indians" hooting around the convoy camp, they became so excited they decided a telegram should be sent off to the War Department. Ike and Brett had some explaining to do to the convoy commander

to see to it the telegram did not go out.* Later, during a card game, the prankster tankers staged a "knife fight" complete with generous dollops of ketchup.

On another occasion, when Brett and Ike and a few officers were driving close to a place where Brett had planted a dead rabbit he and Ike had shot the day before, the boys stopped the car and asked the dudes if they could see the big jack way out there about a hundred yards off. Ashamed to admit they couldn't see it, the easterners agreed they could. At that, Ike unlimbered his Colt .45 and fired once in the

---

* Not so funny. Just in 1916 there had been some tense moments with the Utes. In that year the War Department had to consider the nightmare possibility of three wars: with one of our Indian tribes, with Mexico, and with Germany.

The convoy followed the route of the Lincoln Highway, at that time still more of a dream than a reality. The heavy trucks damaged or destroyed over 80 bridges, all of which had to be repaired before the convoy could continue. In some places the military engineers who accompanied the convoy had to build new bridges.

Dwight D. Eisenhower Library

Coast to Coast with the Doughboys

general direction of the rabbit. The dude officers, themselves aware of how difficult it is to attain accuracy with a Colt .45, were dumbfounded when Brett strolled out and carried back the dead rabbit. Thanks to Eisenhower and Brett, some officers on the expedition were genuinely impressed with the "wildness" of the Wild West.

You say you had never heard of the Garford truck? Small wonder. Judging by the military reports, it seems likely the men of the military convoy must have wished they hadn't heard of it either. One of the Garfords had to be abandoned, but altogether they qualified as the most repaired machines on the trip. The Standard "B" trucks won fame as the "most towed," but then there were many more of them.

The Militor artillery tractor proved to be the most valuable machine in the column. The Macks suffered from great water consumption and weak clutches. The Cadillacs were good except for their timing chains, which tended to stretch. The Dodge tourers proved quite satisfactory (as they had in Mexico and in France). The Rikers, another machine long since lost in automotive history, proved to be the most reliable.

The convoy rumbled into San Francisco on September 6th, 62 days out of Washington, D.C., and, after the most extraordinary efforts, just a few days behind schedule. What they had proved was that it was next door to impossible to move a column of heavy vehicles across the country given the then existing road conditions. Five hundred miles of the trip had been over the most primitive of roads. But it was noted that by the time the boys got to California they were all pretty good drivers. Small wonder. Only twenty-one men had fallen out because of sickness or injuries, and there were no deaths, which in itself

Of the 3,251 miles driven by the convoy, 1,778 miles were driven over dirt roads, mud, sand, mere paths, and in one place an abandoned railroad line. About 500 miles were driven over the most minimal trails. On one in Utah some trucks sank several feet into quicksand and were recovered only after extensive excavations.   Dwight D. Eisenhower Library

Coast to Coast with the Doughboys

In this photo, the boys are scooping up some lemonade donated by citizens of a Western town. No doubt they used all they got; everybody with the column, no matter what his rank, had to get down and push and pull and shovel. Maintaining their schedule, the men worked 16 to 24 hours a day. They arrived in San Francisco just four days behind schedule. They had learned that it was almost impossible to move such a convoy across the U.S. on our poor roads. The first military motor convoy was dramatic proof of the poor quality of our highways.
Dwight D. Eisenhower Library

was probably at least a second degree miracle. One of the nine vehicles that didn't survive the expedition was destroyed when it rolled over and over down the side of a mountain.

The men had to hear yet more speeches when the Willys-Overland Company gave them a dinner in San Francisco. They had fried chicken, hot rolls, corn on the cob, and roast sweet potatoes while they listened to music by the San Francisco Jazz Trio, The Royal Hawaiians, and The Whistling Doughboy. The evening ended with a songfest, and all those hearty young voices rose to belt out favorite wartime ditties such as "Pack Up Your Troubles In Your Old Kit Bag" and

"There's A Long, Long Trail":

"There's a long, long trail a-winding Into the land of my dreams. . ."

But that wasn't the end of the story. Road development in America took a big leap forward in 1956 when Congress provided for the construction of 41,000 miles of toll-free express highways. The Interstate Highway Act of 1956 was signed by President Dwight Eisenhower, who, many years before, had been "impressed" by the necessity of good roads for economic and military purposes.

Vehicles of the First Transcontinental Military Convoy

2 Cadillac tourers
6 Dodge tourers
2 White observation cars
1 White recon car
14 Standard "B" cargo trucks
1 Standard "B" machine shop truck
2 Standard "B" spare parts trucks
2 Standard "B" gasoline tankers
1 Standard "B" water tanker
1 Cadillac searchlight truck
4 Dodge light delivery trucks
3 F.W.D. cargo trucks
3 Garford cargo trucks

2 G.M.C. ambulance trailers
5 G.M.C. ambulances
2 G.M.C. cargo trucks
1 Mack machine shop truck
1 Mack blacksmith shop truck
3 Mack cargo trucks
3 Packard cargo trucks
3 Riker cargo trucks
2 Trailmobile kitchens
3 White cargo trucks
5 Harley-Davidson motorcycles
4 Indian motorcycles
2 tractors

The number of vehicles in the convoy varies slightly from report to report, but that may be because some officers included trailers as vehicles. In any event, over eighty machines were included in the convoy. Not all of them are listed here because several "mystery cars" accompanied the expedition, new models donated by the manufacturers, automobiles that had not yet been released for sale to the public. Willys-Overland sent automobiles along and at least one Packard Twin-Six shows up in photographs. None of the mystery cars appears on any list of convoy vehicles, nor was their performance evaluated by the military personnel.

Judging by the tourists who are inspecting the aeroplanes, these machines must be in Columbus, New Mexico. Below, aviators of the 1st Aero Squadron (left to right), Lt. Bowen, Lt. Carberry, Lt. Chapman, Capt. Foulois, Lt. Milling, and Lt. Rader.

War: Wings Across the Border

HE LAST CAVALRY CAMPAIGN of the U.S. Army had more than one twentieth century wrinkle. While the wheels of the truck trains rolled across the border, the wings of the First Aero Squadron, the entire American "air force" at the time, flew over it. The very first aggressive air sortie of the U.S. Army was flown on the 16th of March when Jenny #44 crossed into Mexico on a reconnaissance mission. Captain T. F. Dodd was at the controls, Captain B. D. Foulois, squadron commander, rode along as observer. The Jenny bounced across the field just south of Columbus, lifted into the air, and droned low and slow into Mexico. This first combat airstrip of the U.S. Army lies just east of the road going south out of Columbus to Palomas, just across the road from Pancho Villa State Park. The area is now covered with mesquite but is commemorated by a sign in the park. Dodd and Foulois returned and landed successfully without anything of great moment to report.

The First Aero Squadron was part of the Signal Corps. It had been established in 1913 and trained at North Island, California, at the Navy and Curtiss Flying School. When ordered to Columbus on the 12th of March, the squadron included 11 pilot officers; one medical officer; 84 enlisted men, drivers, cooks, mechanics, riggers; one civilian mechanic (probably from the Curtiss company), eight Curtiss JN4s, and a dozen trucks and one automobile. The Squadron had been on maneuvers in Texas and Oklahoma; the airplanes were not in first-rate condition, but they were the only operational airplanes the Signal Corps owned.

The Jenny (Curtiss JN4) was one of the world's more unlikely combat aircraft in 1916, but a comparison with European combat aircraft of the day is necessary to show just how far behind the Europeans the Americans had fallen. The Jenny was "powered" by the OX-5, a V-8, water-cooled engine that weighed 390 pounds and turned up 90 h.p. at 1400 rpm. Well tuned, the OX-5 could cause the Jenny to streak through the air at 75 mph. Wing span 43 feet, length 27 feet four inches, height 10 feet six inches. Landing speed about 45 mph. The original Jennys to reach the border were unarmed and were intended for reconnaissance and observation work. General Pershing had hoped they would be able to scout a lot of country in a hurry and possibly find Pancho Villa and his raiders.

The French Spad 7 reached the Western Front in France in 1916. The Spad was a single-seat fighter, one of the best of WWI, and is associated with some of France's highest-scoring pilots. Eddie Rickenbacker flew a Spad, although a later version of the Spad 7. The Spad was also powered by a V-8, in this case the Hispano-Suiza. The classic Hispano-Suiza engine allowed the Spad to climb to 6500 feet in *eight* minutes and do 115 mph at that altitude (later models would do 125 mph). The Spad's two machine guns were synchronized to fire through the propeller. The Spad 7 is a reasonably representative fighter of that period of the war.

The First Aero Squadron would not have lasted ten minutes over the Western Front. The Jenny was even slower than the British R. E. 8, the "Harry Tate," an airplane that flew at the front until the end of the war, mainly because so many of them were built. Many brave men died in R. E. 8s, ten pilots from one squadron in one day.

A lot of Jennys were built, too, but they served as trainers. They were easy to fly. The Jenny's use in Mexico was its one introduction to hostile territory. Ironically, although outclassed by most of the combat aircraft of WWI, the Jenny continued to fly on well into the 1920s with the barnstormers. Lindbergh owned one. It was the Jenny that flew in and out of rough fields all over the country at county fairs, introducing America to aviation.

Meanwhile, back at the border. The squadron was ordered to fly to Casas Grandes, Chihuahua, on March 19th, and so the entire American air force took off at 5:10 p.m. and clattered south on the trail of the horse soldiers. (Maybe it would have been a good idea to have started earlier in the day?) One plane turned back with engine trouble, but the rest flew on and became scattered in the gathering dusk. Four of them put down at Ascension, another at Ojo Caliente, one at Janos, but #41 piled up during a landing at Pearson.

Scratch Jenny #41.

The four planes that landed at Ascension were flown into Casas Grandes on the 20th, as was the plane that had returned to Columbus with engine trouble and the machine that had landed at Janos. The pilot of the airplane that crashed near Pearson *walked* to Casas Grandes. His machine was stripped later for parts, although the motorized detachment sent out to do the job was fired upon by Mexicans. The Jenny that landed at Ojo Caliente was so badly damaged that several days were required to repair it sufficiently to fly it into Casas Grandes.

With six airplanes at the front, a recon was ordered south toward Cumbres Pass, into the Sierra Madres, in order to locate some American troops moving south toward Lake Babicora. Dodd and Foulois took off in 44 at noon on the 20th and headed south out of Casas Grandes.

Whatever Pershing had expected from the aviators and their machines, he was going to be at least partly disappointed. Dodd and Foulois were able to go just twenty-five miles on their mission. As they tried to gain the pass, their machine was forced back time after time by strong air currents. They fluttered just above the pines, the OX-5 roaring impotently at the Sierra Madre foothills. Cumbres Pass lay at 12,000 feet. The Jennys would not climb over 10,000! Disappointed, the men flew back to Casas Grandes to report to Pershing . . . who was also disappointed, to say the least. The first mission a failure. Not only that, but the first flight pointed out that the airplanes on hand were not capable of doing the work proposed for them.

Most of the fields from which the men of the First Aero Squadron flew lay 4,000 to 5,000 feet above sea level. The airplanes would not rise above 10,000 feet, so their area of operations was limited. And March and April are windy months. Caught in a strong head wind, a Jenny could appear to be standing still in the air. Underpowered and with a large wing surface, sudden shifts of wind could be disastrous for them. Lieutenant T.S. Bowen, attempting to land after another flight later in the day on the 21st, was caught in a whirlwind and his machine was rolled up in a ball of shattered wood and torn fabric. Bowen emerged from the debris with a busted nose (a common injury among early fliers) and other minor injuries.

Score: Mexican boondocks, 2; First Aero Squadron, 0.

It was decided that if the Jennys were no good for reconnaissance, they might prove of some use in communicating quickly with the widely separated cavalry columns. With this in mind, two Jennys took off from Casas Grandes on the 21st headed for the Galeana Valley to locate a cavalry column. Dodd, pilot, and Foulois, observer, flew in 44. The Jenny swooped into the Galeana Valley and set down near Galera Lopena, having easily located the troops, who were under the command of Colonel Erwin.

One can imagine the thoughts that must have gone through the heads of some of the older cavalry troopers, a few of whom had served in campaigns against Indians, when they saw the Jenny fluttering down out of the blue. For many of the men, it was their first sight of a real airplane. Here is the link between the hard-riding horse soldiers of the Indian Wars and the long line of men who have fought through the wars of the twentieth century.

The fliers dropped off their message and received a message for delivery back at Casas Grandes. A supply column was sent out to meet the cavalry column. Success. The damned flying machines were good for something after all.

Two missions flew on the 22nd of March. Jennys 42 and 45 were flown into the Galeana Valley to locate some other troops. This flight was a success. The other flight, in 44 and 53, headed south along the Mexican Northwestern Railroad in an attempt to find some troops that were supposed to be moving in that direction. The two machines penetrated the Sierra Madre Mountains as far as the northern end of the railroad tunnel in Cumbres Pass, but here they ran into the same strong winds Dodd and Foulois had encountered on the 20th. Forced almost into the trees, the pilots gave up and returned to Colonia Dublan.

As a result of the failures, Captain Fulois put in a request for more airplanes, more powerful machines, airplanes to come with plenty of spare parts, one extra engine per every two airplanes, two spare propellers, one set of lower wings with wires and fittings, one complete landing gear, an extra set of tail control surfaces with wires and fittings, three spare radiators, three spare magnetos. Captain Foulois had discovered that active campaigning is hard on machines. Those original Jennys weren't new, and the harsh climate of spring-

One of the Jennys that flew into Mexico. This flying machine could pass through the air at 75 mph and climb to 10,000 feet, not good enough for the extreme conditions encountered in Mexico. **Columbus Historical Society**

time northern Mexico was hard on the wood and fabric machines.

On the 23rd a flight of three Jennys dropped into the Galeana Valley again and landed at El Valle to report to Colonel Dodd. But if the old horse soldier had a message to send back, he was out of luck; the aviators were grounded there until the 25th by high winds, dust, and snow. No doubt the cavalry was fully operational in spite of the weather. One shudders at the thought of the ribbing the aviators and their cockeyed flying machines must have taken from the cavalrymen in those two days.

During the next week or so, the aviators turned in some good work. They were needed. The telegraph lines were too easily put out of action and the primitive radios did not always work. Communications by automobile and motorcycle could be slow and, given the frailties of those machines too, not always certain. Between March 26th and April 4th the First Aero Squadron flew seventy-nine missions, carrying mail and dispatches between Columbus, New Mexico, and several points south of the border, all of the flights successful. They were learning, although on the 31st of March rain, hail, and snowstorms forced some of the pilots to land until bad weather had passed by. A wet engine in a Jenny would often start missing. Unable to rise above the weather, the pilots had no choice but to risk a landing—wherever—and wait out the storm, huddled under their airplanes, hoping no Mexicans would appear out of the flying grit.

Old 44 was wiped out on the 6th of April. Carrying mail and dispatches from Namiquipa and Cusihuirachic, it crashed upon landing at San Geronimo. Useful parts were stripped on the spot, the rest was burned. Three down, five to go.

On April 7th, Jennys 43 and 45 were flown to Chihuahua City with duplicate dispatches for the American consul there, Lieutenants Dargue and Carberry piloting, Captains Dodd and Foulois occupying the front cockpits as observers. Unlike the European custom, learned from hard experience in a dangerous sky, where observers occupied the rear cockpits, the Jennys carried their pilots in the rear. There was some nervousness in the squadron about this arrangement; in a crash back in the States one of the squadron's men had died with a hot OX-5 in his lap.

Each plane carried some of the dispatches. Dargue and Foulois, in 43, landed on the south side of town, Carberry and Dodd on the north side. Foulois told Dargue to fly over to the north side of town too, and he started hiking into town with his dispatches. Just as Dargue was taxiing into position for a takeoff, four *rurales* (rural policemen) started firing at the plane. Foulois, little daunted by a little rifle fire, proceeded toward the Mexicans to tell them to cease fire. Instead of following his advice, the *rurales* arrested him. Dargue managed to get off, but Foulois was taken to the city jail, followed by a crowd of many angry men and boys. If Foulois had any doubts about how the Mexicans felt about gringo troops before his arrival in Chihuahua City, the entire matter was set straight for him then and there. Luckily, he managed to tell another American he saw in the street to get word of his predicament to the American consul, to tell the consul to get protection for the aviators and the airplanes.

Dargue flew across town and landed next to 45. Cap-

On April 7, 1916, Lt. H.A. Dargue poses next to his Jenny at Chihuahua City. Reportedly he kept posing for the Mexican photographer in order to keep the crowd from stoning him and his airplane. Jenny No. 43 was later lost in a crash. **U.S. Air Force Academy**

tain Dodd went into town with his dispatches, leaving Lt. Carberry and Dargue with the Jennys. A crowd of Mexicans gathered around the two Jennys, Carranzista soldiers and officers, civilian men of all ages. They insulted the Americans in terms the aviators could easily understand. They burned holes in the airplanes with cigarettes and slashed at the fabric with knives, and they even managed to remove some nuts and bolts from both machines.

Dargue and Carberry decided that before they, too, were taken apart they had better remove themselves and their airplanes from temptation. They got the engines started and the Mexicans retreated as the props kicked up dirt in their faces. They took off in a shower of stones and rocks, the Mexicans running down the field alongside their planes as they gathered enough speed to hop into the air and away from the angry crowd. Carberry flew away and landed at the American Refining and Smelting Company, some six miles away, but as Dargue gained altitude the top section of his fuselage

flew off, damaging the stabilizer as it sailed away. Managing to keep the Jenny under control by some very clever flying, Dargue set the airplane on the ground again in the face of the crowd of Mexicans. Drawing his pistol, he decided to sell himself dearly. . .

Meanwhile, Captain Foulois was able to get himself released by getting in touch with a Colonel Miranda, Chief of Staff to General Gutierrez, Military governor of Chihuahua. Foulois was released and Colonel Miranda sent a guard of troops out to the airplanes, the Mexican guard arriving in time to save Lt. Dargue and his Jenny from destruction. The men spent the rest of the day repairing damage to the two airplanes, and the next day they flew to San Geronimo with dispatches from the American consul to General Pershing. And so the most touch and go incident of the First Aero Squadron during the Punitive Expedition came to a happy end.

Incapable of taking on an active hostile role in the expedition, the Jennys and their aviators continued to turn in some good days by acting as dispatch carriers. On April 11th Lieutenants Dargue and Gorell flew from San Antonio, Mexico, all the way back to the main base at Columbus, New Mexico, a flight of 315 miles, with only one stop at Colonia Dublan. On that same day, Lt. Chapman, alone in 53, landed at Santa Rosalia, south of Chihuahua City, during a reconnaissance flight. He was captured by Carranzista troops and taken to their commander. Later released to continue his flight, Chapman discovered upon returning to 53 that his field glasses, goggles, and some ammunition had been stolen. He was undoubtedly lucky nothing else disappeared.

The Jennys aged fast during the expedition. They were flown almost daily, as long as weather permitted, and they had no cover when they were not in use. The mechanics and riggers kept patching them, using parts from wrecked machines, but after just a few weeks of

Captain Foulois, left, and Captain Dodd, the first two American aviators to make an "aggressive" flight. On March 16, 1916, they flew 20 miles into Mexico to locate U.S. troops. The flight lasted 51 minutes.
U.S. Air Force Academy

A daring young man and his flying machine; Captain B.D. Foulois, commander of the 1st Aero Squadron. Jenny No. 42 turned in some good work until April 14, 1916, when, worn out, it was condemned, dismantled, and destroyed.
U.S. Air Force Academy

active campaigning, the Jennys were definitely wobbly.

Lieutenant Rader wrecked 52 during a recon flight south from Satevo toward Parral. He located Major Howze's command of cavalry near Ojito and tried to land. Unfortunately the ground was rougher than it had looked from the air and he piled up. Taking what he could carry from the Jenny, he set a match to it and then hiked to Howze's column. Presumably he was given a horse to ride. He was over a hundred miles from the nearest base.

Did Rader have his campaign hat with him? The aviators did not look unlike the cavalrymen in their campaign hats and leather puttees. They wore leather jackets when flying and also exchanged their wide-brimmed hats for flying caps and goggles, but other than that they were indistinguishable from anybody else on the expedition.

The expedition's long distance pilot, Lt. Dargue, logged 415 miles on the 15th of April, flying from Columbus to Boca Grande, Pulpit Pass, Dublan, Namiquipa, and Satevo. Four hundred and fifteen miles in one day. The cavalrymen had always been the eyes and ears of the army; one wonders how many of them realized their days in the saddle were numbered.

Also, on the 15th, #42 was condemned. It was dismantled and what couldn't be used on other aircraft was destroyed. The lower wings of 42 were installed on 45 to replace the wings that had been slashed and peppered by cigarette butts in Chihuahua City on the 7th.

U.S. air strength was down to three shaky Jennys, and on the 19th #43 was wrecked when its engine stopped over rugged terrain north of Chihuahua City. Lieutenant Dargue was piloting, Captain R. E. Willis in the front cockpit. It should be remembered that 43 was the other plane that flew into Chihuahua City on the 7th, and it was 43 that Dargue piloted on his remarkably long hops. Apparently 43 had had enough.

Dargue and Willis were reconnoitering and photographing roads in and around Chihuahua City when suddenly all they could hear was the singing of the wind through the struts and wires. The tired OX-5 had given up the ghost. With no *good* places to land below them, Dargue did the best he could. Still, it was a bad wreck. Dargue climbed out unhurt, but Willis, in the hated front cockpit, suffered a severe head wound as well as injuries to his legs and ankles. Dargue had to pull the captain out of the wrecked Jenny. While Willis rested, Dargue recovered their personal gear from the machine. Then he torched the Jenny. They moved away from the burning ship as quickly as they could to avoid any armed Mexicans who might see the smoke rising.

The nearest base, San Antonio, lay sixty-five miles away. With Dargue helping the injured Willis, the two men hiked to San Antonio, suffering terribly on the way from lack of food and water. After Willis had been patched up and the two men had rested, they were driven to Namiquipa in order to report to General Pershing the results of their mission. Better late than never.

Two Jennys left out of the original eight. They were examined on the 20th of April and declared unserviceable for further use in the field. They were flown back to Columbus, stripped, and burned. The rest of the squadron personnel drove back to Columbus to be equipped with new flying machines. It had taken just a month to put the Aviation Section of the Signal Corps out of action. The men settled into Columbus to relax, clean up what gear remained to them, and to await the arrival of new airplanes.

The new machines, when they arrived, turned out to be Curtiss R-2s. Two of them came in on the first of May, and by the end of the month ten more R-2s had shown up. Four airplanes had been awaiting them in Columbus when the squadron pulled in there from Mexico, but tests with the new machines indicated they would most probably be of little use south of the border. Trying to get the squadron into the air again, the men encountered constant trouble with the props, engine failures, and faulty construction of the airplanes themselves.

The Curtiss Aeroplane Company sent a few men to the border to make up new props on the spot. The region was simply too arid; the props cracked in the dry air, so local woods were tried out, with some success. While the propeller problem and other mechanical defects were being worked out, the new planes were fitted out with Lewis guns, a fairly light, air-cooled machine gun then much in use in Europe. Brock Automatic Cameras for aerial photography showed up in Columbus. These were used with some success. Still hardly comparable with anything then going on in Europe on the Western Front, the First Aero Squadron was doing what it could, with what it had, to shape itself into a combat flying group. Luck was with them; the Mexicans didn't have any airplanes of their own!

As has already been noted, the U.S. troops retired to bases in the north of Chihuahua after the period of active pursuit, which had lasted only about two months. While the diplomats wrangled, the Americans did what they could to patrol the north of Chihuahua while at the same time staying out of trouble. The First Aero Squadron continued to fly, but it would be tedious to examine all of their flights here. That first month, when American aviators flew totally inappropriate machines into a veritable wilderness, is the most interesting period, the period when U.S. military aviation was introduced to the real world.

Well, the aviators didn't find Pancho Villa. Nobody else did, either. The "lion of the north" was also the original desert fox. Operating on his own turf, among people who resented the Carranzistas almost as much as the invading gringos, Villa knew how to keep a low profile when the exigencies of revolution and counter revolution indicated that was necessary.

But the aviators turned in some good work. During the spring and summer of 1916 they made 540 flights with a total of over 345 hours in the air, and they covered about 20,000 miles, for an average of about thirty-seven miles per flight. Truly remarkable is the fact that none of the pilots was killed, and what injuries they did suffer were minor. Considering the equipment they were flying, and the terrain they were flying over, that seems to add up to a measure of success.

Certainly the accomplishments of the squadron's ground personnel should be remembered. They kept the airplanes in the air until they were too dangerous to fly. They put trucks together for the rest of the expedition, and they repaired vehicles and trained drivers. They even hauled supplies in their own trucks when they weren't otherwise occupied. The few men of the First Aero Squadron, at work in the U.S. Army's first twentieth century military campaign, were of inestimable value to the success of the expedition.

Was the Punitive Expedition a success? It was thought so at the time, although the press kept carping about the fact that Pancho Villa was not captured. The cavalry was successful in every engagement with Villa's men, and never again did he approach the border with an armed force. He had learned his lesson.

Ironically, it took a Mexican guerrilla fighter to goad the United States into a more heightened degree of readiness for the war in Europe. A cadre of military men was toughened and trained by service in Mexico and along the border, and these men would be on hand to whip into shape the citizen soldiers who went to fight in France. Many of the men who had struggled in the wilderness with flimsy aircraft and recalcitrant motor vehicles soon found themselves Over There.

The last trooper out of Mexico walked his mount into Columbus on the 5th of February, 1917. The border was reasonably secure. Two months later, in April, the United States declared war on Germany. Any interest in the Punitive Expedition was soon overwhelmed by America's involvement in the World War. The Punitive Expedition, the hinge upon which the U.S. Army swung into the age of total war, remains among the haziest of our military memories.

These heavily armed troopers are guarding a Jenny in Mexico. The photo is from the collection of W.M. Ford, the man on the right.
Arizona Historical Society Library/Tucson

One of the most unusual "windsocks" in the United States, this full-sized replica of a Curtiss Jenny is located at the small airfield just north of Columbus, New Mexico. It is framed of steel and sheathed with copper, and is perched on top of a tall, concrete column. The "pilot" was modeled from photos of Captain Foulois, commander of the 1st Aero Squadron. **Albert Manchester**

This adobe structure was once the Adjutant General's Office of Camp Furlong, which is now Pancho Villa State Park. Located next to Columbus, a traveler can put down stakes at the park; one camping spot is right behind the old office. Photo from 1986. **Albert Manchester**

A 1986 photo taken from the top of Cootes Hill, just southwest of Columbus, New Mexico. The railroad station, now a museum, is on the far right. **Albert Manchester**

Columbus Today

The railroad depot at Columbus is now a small museum exhibiting relics from the 1916-1917 period. The railroad tracks are now gone, and plans are going forth to make a good auto road from El Paso to Columbus along the old railroad bed.
Albert Manchester

This is the railroad bed heading west out of Columbus, as seen in 1986. The roadbed to the east, headed towards El Paso, is being converted to a gravel road. **Albert Manchester**

One of several tunnels on the Corley Mountain Highway in Colorado, built on the roadbed of the Colorado Springs-Cripple Creek District Railroad. The Corley Mountain Highway was operated as a toll road from 1924 to 1939, when it became a free public highway known as the Gold Camp Road.

Pikes Peak Library District

The Tourist – Part Two

HE PERIOD from 1919, when Johnny came marching home again, until 1929 or 1930, could easily be called the Golden Age of Motoring. Even if Johnny couldn't buy a legal drink, he could certainly buy a car, and a pretty good one at that, a car with an electric starter, lights, horn, and a windshield and maybe even a solid top. By 1920 Americans were traveling three times as many miles in their autos as they were on the railroads, and eight times as many people were using cars for trips as were going by train. Over two million motor vehicles were manufactured in the United States in 1920.

It is estimated that in 1920 eleven out of thirteen cars being operated in the world were in the United States, and twelve out of thirteen of the cars produced in the entire world were being made in the U.S. The state of Michigan had more automobile registrations than England, Kansas more than France. The car had grown from being a plaything (1895-1905), and a luxury (1905-1915), to a more or less accepted necessity of every family that could afford the few hundred dollars a new car might cost; and by 1916, just before the war, a new Model T cost only $360. The production of horse-drawn vehicles dropped by two thirds between 1914 and 1920.

The automobile was largely responsible for the business boom of the 1920s. Automobiles used about ninety percent of the petroleum products we produced, eighty percent of the rubber we imported, twenty percent of the steel we made, seventy-five percent of the glass, and twenty-five percent of the machine tools. If the railroads were losing a lot of passengers, that loss was largely made up by the automobile manufacturers, who, before the days of large scale motor trucking, used the railroads for shipping all raw materials and the finished product. (Actually, the automobile industry is *still* a major railroad shipper.)

In 1925 the United States produced 3,735,171 passenger cars to drive around on an expanding, improving road system. The Federal Highway Act of 1921 promoted the development of *national* highways, the states receiving money on a fifty-fifty basis to build up thousands of miles of interstate routes. The 1921 highway program also established the numbered highway plan, odd numbers for north-south routes, even numbers for east-west routes. In 1919 Oregon placed a one cent per gallon tax on gasoline, the money to be expended on roads, and by the end of the 1920s every state had a gasoline tax. The automobile culture we live with today was firmly in place by 1930.

The volume of long-distance travel increased during the 1920s, and coast-to-coast runs became commonplace events by 1930. The cars were good, reasonably dependable, and improving all through the decade. Parts, even in remote places, became easy to get. Gasoline was no problem to find. Out on the road, there was still little traffic. A few detractors regretted the sight of

A long, winding climb up the Jerome-Prescott Road in Arizona in the late 1920s. This looks to be a perfectly adequate road for the careful driver.

Arizona Historical Society Library/Tucson

the wide brown cuts across land where just a few years before only a wagon trail had existed, but such people were generally regarded as relics from the last century. There was no hint whatever that the automobile would one day create as many problems as it would solve, that one day we would find ourselves on a treadmill, the economic health of the nation a hostage to the production of automobiles. No, this was the Golden Age. Good cars but not too many of them. Pretty good roads. The country not yet spoiled by strip development along its highways. Just get out on the road and roll through a still relatively pristine countryside.

Although the cars of the 1920s were good, they still had to be *driven*. Roads are so well made today and automobiles so automatic and powerful we've lost something of the intimate relationship one needed with his car. Hills were steeper, curves sharper, engines not so powerful. Gears had to be shifted, and shifted by hand. In an older car you were aware of the machine through the nerve endings of your hands and feet, even your butt. You listened for what the engine would tell you. Was it lugging? Gear down. Each car had its own proper resonance which its owner had to learn. Drivers insen-

sitive to the sound and feel of their machines could ruin a good car in short order.

(In 1951, a long time before the Alaska Highway was straightened and leveled, I drove an old Ford to Alaska. Past millions of dark trees, over what seemed like every hill in Canada. One day, way up there someplace in northern B.C., after driving much too long, my mind could no longer tell me whether I was going uphill or downhill. Maybe it was time to stop, but I was only seventeen, and I didn't. So I drove the car simply by the feel of it vibrating through the shifting lever, steering wheel, and seat. Ahead, the road looked level, but I may have been going up or down. I could tell if I looked out the rear window, but I couldn't drive like that, and the rear view mirror told me nothing. Driving by instinct, totally in tune with the machine, shifting gears by the feel and sound it transmitted to me.)

* * *

THE YEAR WAS 1920. Deming, New Mexico, lay a hundred miles away, a day's travel in the desert, and it was already getting on to three o'clock in the afternoon. The car was a Cadillac Eight with two young women on

The road up Lookout Mountain, 15 miles west of Denver. This road no longer exists. The year is 1926; older trails up the mountain are clearly visible. **Shirley Sorenson Collection**

The beginning of the well-known Sorenson Truck Service of Colorado. The first truck owned by the company, it is a 1916 Dearborn Universal Apperson, and was patched together from three vehicles.
Shirley Sorenson Collection

board, Winifred Hawkridge Dixon and Katherine "Toby" Thaxter, of Boston. They had already been lost once that day because Toby had read the directions from the *Colorado* section—instead of the New Mexico section—of the guidebook, and now they had arrived at a place where a windmill stood guard over a fork in the road.

"Pass the windmill to the left," Toby read out of the guidebook.

"Left?" Winifred looked doubtfully at the muddy road to the left of the windmill. A much better road passed to the right of it.

"Left," Toby repeated.

Left it was, but the mud was deeper than it looked and the Cadillac sank . . . and stuck. The car settled to the hubs, to the running boards. The Bostonians dismounted into the muck. As it turned out, the road to the right of the windmill was simply a detour around the mud. Winifred hiked back two miles through the scorching sun to a crossroads. After waiting an hour without a sign of another car, she collected a bunch of white stones and arranged them at the crossroads to form a message which would tell any future passerby that they were up by the windmill and in need of help.

When Winifred walked back to the scene of the disaster, she found the Cadillac partly jacked up but leaning drunkenly, deeper in the mud than ever on one side. Toby was plastered with mud, looking terribly discouraged. It seemed the mudhole was tenanted by at least one head of dead cattle, and smelled like it. Toby had fallen on it, inserting her finger into its eye.

While the girls stood, thirsty, hungry, and dirty, look-

ing at their embarrassed Cadillac, a big youthful cow-poke moseyed by and advised them that a team of horses might be found about two miles southeast. Wini-fred and Toby walked there, only to find the house empty. Another empty house lay just beyond. As it was now dark, they decided to return to their car for the flashlight, so they could hike the ten miles to the closest town, a dismal place called Rodeo, back on the Arizona-New Mexico border . . .

Winifred and Toby had planned to "drift" around the great Southwest, writing and sketching as they moved from place to place. Since it is impossible to drift when one is tied to train schedules, the idea had occurred to them to drive their own car. Winifred owned a car, she had been driving for some years, and an acquaintance of theirs who had done some driving in the West assured them they should have no trouble.

Furthermore, a AAA map showed confident red lines wherever they might want to go. The map, with its inducement of romantic place names, convinced them; drive they would. They and their car went by sea to Galveston, where the trip started in earnest. Winifred later admitted, in a book she wrote called *Westward Hoboes*, that had she known what they were in for, she never would have undertaken the motor trip.

Westward Hoboes, published in 1922, is a classic among tales of early motoring. Because they were not simply intent upon getting from one place to another, and indeed did drift about, as far as one was able to drift in a Cadillac in the desert in 1920, they have left an excellent record of the early days of motoring. This book, now rare, is one of the very best descriptions of a colorful time and place, when a motorist could have traveled many thousands of miles of the West without finding a single drive-up window.

* * *

When Toby and Winifred got within sight of their car they saw another car parked by the windmill, its two occupants waiting for them to return. The men were armed with rifles and revolvers, and both wore cartridge belts. They waited because they had noticed that the luggage in the Cadillac probably belonged to women, and they had been waiting for two hours for the occupants of the car to return, a kindness Winifred thought would be unusual east of Chicago. The men spent the next hour shoveling the car free and pulling it to firm ground.

The girls drove over 11,000 miles during their tour of the West, crisscrossing New Mexico, Arizona, and then climbing up through Utah, through Idaho, Montana, and then across the northern states to the East Coast. They stuck fast in mud in every state they crossed, paid 50¢ for a gallon of gas in the more remote towns, sometimes a quarter to get a tire repaired, sometimes nothing, if they happened to be buying gasoline at the same time. Cattlegates, often several in a single mile, slowed them down. But being Easterners, they felt for the first time in their lives they had all the room they needed.

Dressed in yellow goggles and khaki outfits, they fixed tires peppered by horseshoe nails and broken whiskey bottles. They figured to average twenty miles per hour between places, if they were lucky, and they learned to shift down quickly when they noticed the car lugging in sand.

One interesting aspect of traveling at this time was the necessity of carrying enough cash to get one by for at least several days. Many travelers carried large sums of money, as there were no credit cards, and cashing a personal check several states west of one's hometown bank was an unlikely achievement. A local bank could wire the hometown bank, or a certified check could be mailed to a post office en route, but most travelers settled for carrying plenty of money, because they could never tell when they might have to use a big bunch of it all at once.

In spite of the lower wages of 1920, parts for a car could cost almost as much as an equivalent part would cost today. A battery sold for thirty to thirty-five dollars, tires twenty-five to thirty-five dollars, and gasoline varied greatly in price. The Barrus party, which crossed the country in 1920 (see below), spent a little over 31¢ as an average, but had to spend 60¢ in New Mexico. Expensive for the time, considering the Oldsmobile they were driving got only 11.3 miles to the gallon. Cars of the period tended to burn much more oil than cars we know today, and oil could cost from 15 to 35¢ per quart. Gasoline, it should be noted, might be dirty and of poor quality, necessitating repairs a little way down the road.

Most travel writers of the day recommended leaving most of one's clothes at home and taking along just a couple of khaki outfits for each passenger, with, if thought truly necessary, one more or less formal outfit. Winifred and Toby settled for khaki. Significantly, dust and dried mud are just about the same color as khaki. Many early wilderness drivers wore high laced boots or leather leggings, and, man or woman, nobody was seen outdoors without a hat. As many of the cars of the 1920s were still open tourers, driving goggles were still needed.

The women motorists would put up at the minimal hotels if they had to, but they discovered camping out on the desert was a cleaner experience. Now and then they would stop in the town auto parks, but the intimacy of such places was too unsavory for the Bostonians. Cabins for motorists were still rare in 1920, although

A farm family poses in front of the family flivver in the 1920s. The family auto served as a backdrop for photos as soon as it could be driven in front of the scenery. **Albert Manchester Collection**

during the decade such establishments would become fairly easy to find, and by 1930 the larger cities would be able to boast establishments easily recognizable as motels. If motorists' cabins did not have private baths, tourists were advised to inspect the public baths before putting their money down.

In the White Mountains of Arizona, home of the White River Apaches, Winifred and Toby, afraid to camp out, begged for room and board at a cavalry post, Fort Apache. Being the only "inn" in the region, the few travelers through the area were always directed to Fort Apache, where the U.S. government put them up . . . for a price.

* * *

WHILE TOBY AND WINIFRED were rattling around the West with no particular destination in mind, another traveler who knew even less about cars than they did was trying to drive his family home to New York from California. M.F. Barrus was a professor of botany at Cornell University who had gone out to California to study while he was on his sabbatical. There, he was bitten by the automobile bug so badly that he bought a used 1916 V-8 Oldsmobile which sported wire wheels and was painted a delicate blue. He paid $1,000 for a car with almost 5,000 miles on the clock. A new Olds would have cost just a few hundred more, and anybody who knew anything about used cars would have questioned 5,000 miles in four years, even if the car had been owned by the legendary schoolteacher who drove it only on Sundays, and then just to church.

Although Barrus could not drive, he proposed to drive his Olds all the way across the United States with his wife, two children, and a secretary, visiting friends en route and stopping along the way to gather bits of flora, an especially attractive example of *Chrysanthemum leucanthemum*, for example.

Professor Barrus was, however, wise enough to buy the car somewhat in advance of the trip so that he could learn to drive and become familiar with his family's first car. It was a good thing he did, because before they started across the continent the car had to be treated to a complete engine overhaul (5,000 miles?).

Just the automobile cost of the trip to Ithaca, New York, was $454.95. This may not seem like a lot now, but considering the professor was making only $3,500 per year, it becomes apparent an automobile adventure in the 1920s could be a fairly hefty investment. Average cost of gasoline was 31.1¢, reaching a high of 60¢ in New Mexico. Including two oil changes, they used fourteen *gallons* of oil. On the trip, the heavily loaded machine got only 11.3 miles to the gallon. The car overheated several hundred times, the springs broke many times until new springs had to be purchased, a valve spring broke, the radiator sprung a leak, the feed pipe to the carb kept breaking, and the carb had to be cleaned.

This litany ignores the constant tire trouble they experienced. Luckily, they had no "major" problems. (The combination of just a few such problems would spoil any trip for a modern motorist.) The Barrus transcontinental expedition took fifty-five days, which included nine days for repairs and visiting friends.

Because the car was carrying so much weight, Barrus did not take along many recommended items, such as block and tackle. He made it without such tools, his passengers getting out to walk up steep hills and through sandy places, pushing the car when they had to.

Considering the cost of long trips, it is little wonder cross-country motoring took many years to become a national sport. Few citizens made as much money as did Professor Barrus, and fewer still were lucky enough to get a month or two off from work or away from their business. Such trips were just too much of an investment in time and money for most Americans.

However, as rare as transcontinental motoring was even by 1920, the *Ithaca Journal News* did not bother reporting the event. We can assume motoring adventures into the dark heartland of America had become commonplace enough so they were no longer newsworthy, at least not in Ithaca.

Most of the motorists who had to cross the western states back then agreed unless one truly loved to motor under the most trying conditions, a better bet would have been to take the train. This held true until about 1930, although of course roads in one section could be better than in another section at any given time. We have forgotten that dirt roads and gravel roads were only as good as local road repair people were willing to make them. During one motorcycle trip through Alaska, I remember encountering a section of a gravel road that had been graded by an artist. He *must* have been an artist. Never again did I encounter a gravel road as smooth. I kicked my old Harley up as fast as it would go, a little over fifty, and I leaned back and forth into the curves. Earlier in the day I had pounded north over a bit of the Richardson Highway that was so rough it had quite worn me out just trying to keep the wheel pointing down the road at about twenty mph. Traveling off pavement was always a matter of luck, motorists' roulette.

* * *

THE TERM "Roaring Twenties" did not refer to all the cars in America at the time, but it could have. By the end of the decade we had over twenty-two million cars registered. Many of them were penetrating the Rockies and the deserts, and up there in Colorado Springs Spencer Penrose was shopping around for a fleet of new cars to run on his Pikes Peak Auto Highway.

After the Pikes Peak road was opened to general traffic, Spencer Penrose bought some White twelve-passenger vehicles and some White Six automobiles to haul tourists to the crest. However, by the early 1920s those first vehicles were worn out and outmoded. The affluent tourists arriving in Colorado Springs on the crest of the business boom expected jazzier modes of transportation. The management at the Broadmoor Hotel looked for a suitable replacement and their critical gaze fell on the Pierce-Arrow.

Why the Pierce?

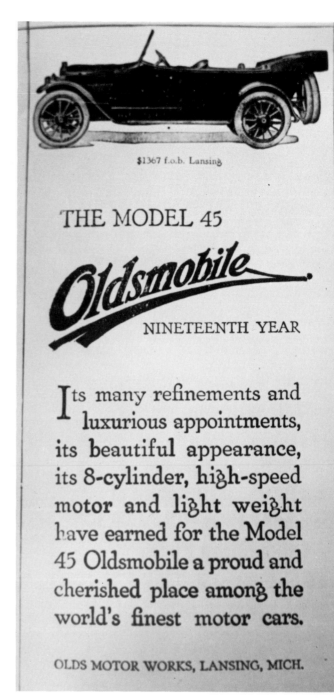

$1367 f.o.b. Lansing

THE MODEL 45

Oldsmobile

NINETEENTH YEAR

Its many refinements and luxurious appointments, its beautiful appearance, its 8-cylinder, high-speed motor and light weight have earned for the Model 45 Oldsmobile a proud and cherished place among the world's finest motor cars.

OLDS MOTOR WORKS, LANSING, MICH.

This Model 45 Olds is the same car the Barrus party drove across the country in 1920. Theirs was a 1916 model; the car pictured is a 1917 model. Cars did not change a great deal from year to year until about 1920. **Albert Manchester Collection**

"They were one of the best cars on the road in them days," claimed Fred Brothers, who was Transportation Manager for the Broadmoor Hotel in 1982. Fred had been working for the Broadmoor since the hotel opened in 1918, first as an elevator operator, then, within six months, as a mechanic-trainee in the garage. He had checked out a lot of cars in six decades; he had a right to his automotive opinions. "The Pierce-Arrows were well built and they just didn't give us any trouble. The tourists liked them. The saying was that the Pierce rode as smooth as a train."

Just possibly the Pierce did ride "as smooth as a train," but they were also manifestly unsuitable as hill climbers.

"They just burned up climbing the mountains," Fred Brothers recalled. "There was a water station every three miles and they'd have to stop at each one to change the water."

Few self-respecting tourists will put up with such time-consuming antics; a way had to be found to get nonboiling Pierce-Arrows all the way up Pikes Peak.

To find the solution to the problem, two top mechanics from the factory in Buffalo, New York, went out to Colorado Springs with a Pierce and a railroad car full of parts.

It was a summer of trial and error for the wizards from New York. The boys ran a standard Pierce-Arrow up the mountain until it boiled over. Then back to the shop. They tore down the machine again and again, always switching parts, experimenting. Then up the mountain again, always that damn mountain.

The Pierce-Arrow had not been designed to climb "hills" like Pikes Peak. Few cars were, especially when loaded with seven passengers, a load which could certainly equal half a ton. The mechanics from the East stayed all summer, but by the time the aspens were shimmering gold in the higher elevations they had built a car that could haul itself onto the 14,110-foot summit without even breaking into a sweat.

Not a very speedy car, to be sure. The main solution to the problem was finding the correct gear ratio. The Series 33 Pikes Peak Pierce-Arrow had a 13/60 rear end ratio (4.61 to 1). They made other changes from the stock car, possibly in the clutch, drive line, and water pump, and the radiators were "quite a bit larger than standard", according to Fred Brothers. The Pikes Peak Pierce utilized a standard three-speed transmission and six-cylinder engine, the Dual-Valve Six. The hood with its fourteen large louvers was considered a high altitude option, standard equipment on Pierce-Arrows sold in the Rocky Mountain states during that era.

Pikes Peak is spectacularly "there," rising regally and virtually alone in its corner of Colorado, a source of legend and superstition to the aboriginal peoples who came into that country, a landmark for Spanish and American explorers . . . and a challenge to almost everybody else who has followed them. Hikes and burro rides were tourist activities in the last decades of the 1800s, and in 1891 a cog railway was completed to the top of the mountain. By the 1920s, almost everyone who summered in Colorado Springs would have to take on the peak. Twenty-five Pierce-Arrows were in the first sale to the Broadmoor, the largest single automobile purchase made in Colorado up to that time. By 1928 the Broadmoor had sixty Pierce-Arrows in service.

The cars could be rented, with a driver, to take the tourist almost anyplace, even as far as Salt Lake City, but most of them were used on Pikes Peak. They weren't pampered. A car might have had to make three

The fleet of new Pierce-Arrows in front of the Broadmoor Hotel in Colorado Springs. When these cars were purchased by the Broadmoor, it was the largest single motor vehicle purchase up to that time.
Broadmoor Hotel

climbs in one day, starting with the "sunrise trip," which was scheduled to put a redoubtable tourist on the crest in time to see the sun come boiling up over the rim of the world. In the 1920s a Pikes Peak trip cost $6.00. To stay warm in the open cars, a tourist could rent a sheepskin coat at the tollgate.

All the drivers were hired locally. Don Lowrie, of Colorado Springs, drove for the Broadmoor in the 1920s. "The head mechanic would take three or four men out who wanted to be drivers for the Broadmoor," Don explained in 1982. "They would go up Pikes Peak and the men would take turns driving. If they drove good enough, they got the job. That's all there was to it."

One fellow didn't even get a chance to drive. Asked by the Broadmoor mechanic if he knew how to double-clutch, the man laughed and said they couldn't kid him, he could see there were only three pedals on the floor, and he knew damn well two of them were for the brake and the gas. He couldn't see two clutch pedals . . .

The Pikes Peak Auto Highway, the "world's highest highway," closes every year on or about the first of October as winter moves down the mountain. In the early days the road was opened every spring for its entire length by pick and shovel, even when drifts gathered to depths of twelve or fifteen feet. In 1926 new snow filled the road as fast as it could be cleared; the first tourist on the peak that year did not arrive until July.

But the season at the lower elevations was much more extended. The Broadmoor's big touring Pierce-Arrows, loaded with swell tourists from all over the country, were common sights in the Pikes Peak region. Regular runs were made to Cheyenne Mountain, Cripple Creek, Seven Falls, The Cave of the Winds, The Garden of the Gods, or wherever a wondering tourist had a hankering to go, even if it was just on a Rocky Mountain picnic after a stop at a grocery store for the makings.

In spite of the dependability and comfort of the Pierce-Arrows, the cars were replaced by Cadillacs in 1932. Nobody remembers why the change was made, unless, as Fred Brothers suggested, the Board of Directors of the Broadmoor had interests in General Motors. They could not have been dissatisfied with the machines; every Pierce-Arrow the Broadmoor put into service in the 1920s was still climbing the mountain in

A supply depot on Pikes Peak during the construction of the highway.

Broadmoor Hotel

A White automobile on Pikes Peak in 1916. The White Company, an early builder of automobiles, worked its way into the building of heavier machines. White makes many heavy trucks for use today. For more early photos of the Pikes Peak Highway, see the end of Chapter Two.
Pikes Peak Library District

1932. Not a single Pierce was sufficiently worn out to be junked, not one had gone out of control in all of those trips on the mountain, nobody had been seriously injured in one of them.

Certainly the Pierce-Arrow Motor Company could have used the business; the company went under in 1938, a victim of the Depression and changing social values. The Pierce-Arrows remain a fine example of American engineering and workmanship. After the cars went out of style, and could be bought for very

little, they were used for many kinds of workhorse jobs: tow trucks, school buses, small trucks, even for running small mills. As recently as 1986, a Pierce-Arrow of about 1926 vintage was found in Kentucky where it had been used to run a small sawmill.

Although the Broadmoor Hotel had the largest fleet of automobiles for hire by the tourists, travelers could also hire cars from the Antlers Hotel or the Colorado Springs Scenic Auto Company. That these businesses could flourish is evidence that most travelers did not

One of the Broadmoor's Pierce-Arrows following a snowplow up the mountain in the spring. Note the distinctive headlamp. **Broadmoor Hotel**

arrive in town with their cars. They arrived by train; they expected to be chauffeured about once they were on the scene. Colorado's fleets of fine touring cars helped open up the West to general tourism.

* * *

In 1917, forty-five years after Yellowstone Park was established as our first national park, an automobile finally poked its radiator into the place. The first car in our first national park. Now, Yellowstone has to contend with over a half million cars and two million visitors per year. But back in the 1920s, when business was described as the business of the nation, road building was considered good for business. By the end of the 1920s virtually every national park could be reached by motorists. Spreading the business around.

In 1927, Colorado's famous road over Trail Ridge was started, a road that would take visitors to Estes Park along a startlingly beautiful drive up to 12,183 feet above sea level. The road was well inserted into the landscape, to make it as unobtrusive as possible. On the other hand, the Cheyenne Mountain Highway just outside of Colorado Springs, completed in 1925 at the cost

of a million dollars, was much resented by the residents for the ugly scar it left across the slopes. Whatever business the new road brought the town was not considered to be worth the marring of such a beautiful mountain. The good sense of many citizens was not entirely connected to their purses.

* * *

If decent night accommodations were a gamble for the early motorists, the victualing stops along the way could be an absolutely frightening experience. A few hamburger stands were popping up along the highways by 1930, but in 1920, and especially in the West, the motorists' gastronomic pleasures were in the hands of whomever was running the town cafe. In many parts of the West this institution was pronounced "calf."

Of course, if a motorist was lucky enough to get to a town with a Harvey House, his food problem was most likely solved. Fred Harvey was an Englishman who traveled across the United States in the late 19th century by train. He was appalled by the food and treatment served out to train travelers of the day, especially in the West. Working with the railroads (mainly the

The fleet of cars belonging to the Antlers Hotel in Colorado Springs. This is the 1920s and most of these cars appear to be Pierce-Arrows. How can you tell? The distinctive headlamp molded into the fender design, the "frog-eye" appearance, and the fact that there is no Pierce-Arrow insignia on the radiators. The cars were used for transporting "dudes" into the wilds. **Pikes Peak Library District**

The Halfway House on Pikes Peak, a resting place on the road. It's spring, but cold, and possibly the tourists have stopped for a warm meal.
Pikes Peak Library District

A load of tourists on Pikes Peak in a Broadmoor Pierce-Arrow. One wonders how often the individual drivers had to pose for such photos.
Broadmoor Hotel

Santa Fe), he established hotels and restaurants along their routes, institutions now forgotten by most Americans who are not familiar with railroading history. Harvey Houses saved generations of Americans from having to eat the most wretched food west of the Mississippi. The Harvey Girls, the restaurant waitresses hired for cleanliness and their cheery faces, put a glint in the eye of many a weary male traveler.

Most towns did not harbor a Harvey House. The local cafe of the 1920s was certainly not a unit in a chain of eateries that served homogeneous cardboard concoctions with cute names, but the traveler did have to have a spirit of adventure when he pushed open the fly-covered screen door. He was surrendering himself and his family to the whimsy of business persons who may or may not have had the best interest of his fellow citizens at heart.

However, the majority of local cafes were probably at least pretty good, although the food served in them tended to be what was seasonal. My friend, Harold Collyer, said that he and Bud generally ordered breakfast, no matter what time of day it was, "because it's harder to mess up breakfast than almost any other meal." Bacon and eggs. Let the locals eat the chicken fried steak, if they have confidence in it. Harold and Bud ate a lot of pie. He told me he could travel around the world eating ham and eggs, fried potatoes, and apple pie. Fried potatoes won't kill you, either.

There wasn't a single hamburger stand between Texas and the Pacific. Very often the boys just cooked out. Build up a fire, punch a few holes in the cans of beans, put them against the fire to heat. Then wrap a rag around the can, cut it open, and spoon out the steaming beans. That and a couple of pieces of jam-covered bread was a meal.

At one small place in Arizona the boys decided to order a big steak each. They had fought through sand all day, they felt they deserved a treat. Harold said the grumpy cuss who ran the cafe, who was cook, waiter and dishwasher, must have been saving those steaks especially for them. The steaks were on the tough side, Harold said, and would have made good tire boots. The boys couldn't chew them, even with their enthusiastic young choppers. The owner of the place refused to cook them anything else, and then disappeared into the kitchen, so Harold and Bud sawed the steaks into pieces and threw them into the kitchen. The cook didn't dare come out. Harold could still raise a chuckle at the memory, almost seventy years after the event.

Up in Utah, however, Winifred Dixon and Toby Thaxter, stopping at an unpainted shack with a sign proclaiming it to be a cafe, were overwhelmed with the amount of good, wholesome food that poured out of the kitchen. All you could eat for six bits. Meat pie, ham, cheese, raspberries, cherries, apple pie and chocolate cake. Country cooking.

Hotels and restaurants were a roll of the dice.

Angelo Cimino races the Broadmoor Hotel's hill climb entry to the top of Pikes Peak, circa 1927; note the railroad pushcar just over the hood of the car.
Broadmoor Hotel

The Harvey House lunchroom at Rincon, New Mexico, circa 1923. Harvey Houses saved generations of Americans from having to eat the most wretched food west of the Mississippi. **Santa Fe Railway**

* * *

By the mid-1920s finding gasoline was no longer a gamble, although the price could vary considerably. Many people gave up carrying extra gasoline, although even as late as 1928 no gas stations could be found between El Paso and Carlsbad, New Mexico, a distance of 165 miles. By 1923 we had gasoline that contained tetraethyl lead to reduce "spark knock" and increase engine efficiency. Gasoline was cleaner than it had been in the 'teens, more uniform from pump to pump. What is generally true throughout most of the history of gasoline manufacturing is that although the price of gasoline did not vary greatly (until recently), the product continued to improve. The distance that one gallon of gasoline would move a ton of automobile continued to increase.

The gasoline station was more of a neighborhood institution than it is now. The owners of gas stations were generally prepared to tackle extensive repairs, and they sold a wider variety of replacement parts than can be found in modern stations. Gasoline stations were dirty, well used places where a fellow could hang out and drink soda pop, where boys could bring their bicycle inner tubes to sink in the tin, water-filled tub outside to find bubbling holes. Inside the gas station, a fellow had to be careful; the grease pit was just that, a greasy pit over which a customer drove his car for servicing. It is not recorded how many people fell into those old traps.

The gas stations of the 'teens sold, besides gasoline, cans of oil and tins of grease. Few early gas stations would change oil or otherwise service a car. In 1910 garages and gas stations accounted for only about forty percent of the gasoline sold, but by 1920 these businesses were selling at least eighty-five percent of the gasoline sold in the United States.

The filling station of the 'teens developed into the service station of the 1920s, which was a combination

The Filling Station

A White truck used by Texaco, circa early 1920s. The White Company had been a manufacturer of automobiles, but they did very well when they decided to concentrate most of their efforts on heavier vehicles. **Texaco**

Through the 1920s the local gas station continued to become more sophisticated. This station, in San Antonio, Texas, is a drive-through from street to street, and is using gas pumps. **Texaco**

By 1930, the gas station had developed into the institution we know today. This is a filling station in Houston in 1931. **Texaco**

Gasoline delivery became increasingly efficient as the demand rose. In 1921, this 3½-ton Mack truck could carry 1,000 gallons. **Texaco**

The Filling Station

This gas station in Houston looks like a temple to the Great God Automobile. The date is about 1929.

Texaco

A beautiful Diamond T truck which could carry 1,500 gallons in five compartments. Such a vehicle would not be out of place today, in spite of the fact that it is a 1932 model. Truck manufacturers are not hampered by the "necessity" of changing styles every year, a habit automobile manufacturers adopted around 1920.

Texaco

filling station and repair shop. This neighborhood business has been phased out in recent years, to be replaced by gasoline stations that provide the simple services of the original filling stations of many years ago. The corner gas station, built to oil company-approved specifications, is a phenomenon that came along in the late 'teens and early 'twenties.

By the mid- to late-'twenties, a motor trip across many parts of the West was feasible for a great many Americans if they had the time and money to invest. If more people weren't taking the risk, it was simply because we had not reached that plateau of national affluence where the majority of the population could afford such an adventure.

But if North America was becoming a motorist's paradise, one continent still remained exceptionally dark as far as the automobile was concerned.

* * *

WITH THE ACQUISITION of German East Africa (Tanganyika) by England after the First World War, the maps of Africa came to display an irregular strip colored Imperial Red all the way from Cape Town to Egypt. It was inevitable that adventurous Englishmen would want to test their mettle—and that of their motor cars—by driving from one end of Africa to the other. Although not the first to have a go at it, the expedition of Major Chaplin Court Treatt and his plucky wife Stella was the first to win through to the end. An earlier adventurer had been killed by a leopard in Rhodesia.

The Court Treatts were not strangers to Africa; Stella came from colonial and pioneer stock on both sides of her family, and Major Court Treatt had been posted to Africa after having been badly injured when, flying as an observer on the Western Front in 1916, his airplane was shot down. He stayed on after the armistice, pre-

paring airstrips for the first trans-Africa airplane flight.

The Royal Flying Corps had used Crossley motor vehicles, so Court Treatt had ample opportunity to determine their characteristics and reliability. (The English Crossley has no relationship whatsoever with the American Crosley.) Also, he came to know a good deal about the African bush and the peoples living in it. All of this experience would prove crucial during the journey north.

Kit and cars were assembled in England and shipped to South Africa. The Crossleys were the 25/30 model, known in the British military as the "25/30 tender." They were powered by an engine that was considered almost indestructible, a notion the Court Treatts should have proven to almost anybody's satisfaction. The Crossley engine was a four-cylinder, in-line, L-head, water-cooled, 4.5-liter side-valver with a five-bearing crankshaft. The Court Treatt machines were modified with light truck bodies.

The 25/30 was originally an automobile, appearing on the roads of England just a few years prior to the First World War, and over the years it changed little except for military and commercial modifications. Three thousand of them were produced every year during the war and they saw action on every front. In Ireland, the 25/30 tenders earned the hatred of the Irish Nationalists . . . there, the machines were the favored transport of the Black-and-Tans.

Their "kit" was everything they thought they might need during a year in the bush, and was limited to one ton per vehicle. Disposing of "necessary" items as they traveled, their kit became progressively lighter as the trail became progressively rougher, until the expedition was skimming along with the barest essentials.

The Court Treatts pulled out of Cape Town on the

Rural Fill-ups

San Ysidro, New Mexico, in the late 1920s. San Ysidro is about 40 miles north of Albuquerque on State Route 44, close to Jemez Pueblo. The gas pump in front of the San Ysidro Trading Co. is typical of the era in places with little or no electricity. Gasoline was pumped into the glass container at the top, then drained by gravity into a waiting car's tank.
Margaret Wennips Moses Collection

The Crossleys are pulled across the Naam River. Early motorists in Africa had hundreds of local citizens to help get them through the rough places; the Court Treatts would not have succeeded without them.

Court Treatt

23rd of September, 1924. With them were Errol Hinds, Stella's youngest brother; T. A. Glover, a photographer; Fred Law, a journalist; and Julius, an African cook. Ahead of them lay the length of the continent, deserts, forests, swamps, lands teeming with wild game and occupied by some tribes that were but marginally tamed. This was adventure in the classic style, and it was a wonderful time to roll slowly through the African back country.

"Slowly" is the word. The season turned out to be unusually rainy. In Rhodesia they "drove" 380 miles in *four months*. They built log roads, stone roads, and roads of brush. Dozens of locals would gather to help them push and pull and dig. Some days two miles was

as far as they could go. At night, with wind and rain buffeting their camp, the adventurers were ankle deep in mud even inside their tents. As they pushed on, they continued to jettison what back in England had seemed absolute necessities. Even food was scrapped, but the expedition was armed with a battery of Rigby rifles, from a .275 to a .475, which could be used to keep the camp pot full.

A trailer was built but soon discarded when it proved impracticable. The metal car roofs, constructed so they could be removed and hooked together for use as a river craft, were left behind. Almost anything not needed for movement toward Egypt was tossed out, much to the delight of the natives. Ducks swam by them on the roads. One stretch, normally a day's run but for the constant rain, took them a month to cover.

Time out was called at Victoria Falls to recuperate and refit. Their reward for having struggled through the water-logged country was to see the falls in all their glory.

Errol Hinds and Major Court Treatt were the mechanics for the Crossleys. By the time they got to Cairo, they must have been among the best mechanics in all of Africa, at least as far as Crossleys are concerned. Considering the treatment the cars had to undergo, it's surprising they simply weren't pulled apart.

Crossing flooded swampland they almost lost one vehicle. They had stopped to fill the radiator and clean the magneto. Gasoline must have overflowed from the carburetor, forming a film on the water. When somebody lit a cigarette and threw the match down, flames shot up all around the car. The engine compartment blazed. They ripped sand and mud from the ground and hurled it on the engine. Court Treatt wrenched a fire extinguisher out of the car and joined the battle. The car was saved.

The expedition rested again in Nairobi, a revelation of civilization, its shop-lined streets crowded with automobiles and fashionably dressed Europeans, a welcome change from the wilderness where the Court Treatt's neighbors wore leaves, ashes, tatoos, or nothing at all . . . and carried long spears with large, sharp blades.

Bridge-building had to be counted among the skills required of the cross-country African motorist of that now-long-ago day. The expedition repaired dozens of flimsy bridges never intended for motor vehicles, raced over teetering structures before they could collapse, or simply called in a hundred or so natives to pull the machines through the water.

In the Sudan, however, the dangerous, mercurial Dinka tribe all but refused to help the travelers—and appeared to be on the verge of mayhem—until Major Court Treatt kicked their stubborn chief into the river the expedition wanted to cross. The other Dinkas decided Court Treatt was a man after their own hearts, and the proud warriors set to work building a bridge over the Bahr el Arab.

It was in the Sudan that the Crossleys became submarine vehicles. Some rivers were too wide and deep to be bridged, so the Crossleys were pulled across under water, an empty gas can tied to the machine and floating on the surface to show its location. Carbs and instruments were removed before each dunking. Once out of the water, the Crossleys were drained. Then, with the transmissions in low gear and with natives pushing and pulling, the vehicles were forced ahead so that the engines would whirl around and pump out the rest of the water. Those old Crossley engines must have been indestructible, considering the residue of river silt that must have remained in them.

A small native war erupted behind them as they drove out of Dinka country, bumping along through deep elephant tracks, across territory their maps indicated to be "uninhabited and unsurveyed." They reached the Nile and rested at Khartoum. Only the wide desert lay ahead on the road to Cairo.

Free at last of swamp and mud, the travelers drove into deep sand. A whole new bag of tricks had to be learned, which included picking up and laying down boards in the softer places, a tedious exercise. They learned, too, to maintain good speed over the thin crust of the desert, fast enough so they would not crack

A crash. This Crossley's brakes slipped on a steep hill and the vehicle careened backwards down the slope until it hit a tree. **Court Treatt**

Major and Stella Court Treatt, outfitted for the African bush. They were the first to win through from Cape Town to Cairo by automobile, in 1924 to 1926. The trip took 16 months. **Court Treatt**

through into the soft sand below. The traditional caravan routes proved impossible, great for camels, terrible for automobiles. Searching for hard ground, wide swings were made into country rarely crossed by the local people. Once sick of the sight of water, they now loaded as much as they could on the cars. But water had to be conserved. Every morning water from Stella's hot water bottle (desert nights can be chilly) was shared around for washing up, brushing teeth, shaves, and then poured into the car radiators.

On and on across the desert, and then one day they spotted the pyramids on the horizon. And so they had made it, Cape to Cairo . . . in *sixteen months*. The battered Crossleys pulled into Cairo where crowds, civilization, and a degree of fame awaited them. Africa, at least in one direction, had been conquered by the automobile. Stella Court Treatt found she was immensely sad; in spite of the work and danger, she was sorry the trip had ended. The Court Treatt's adventure is without a doubt one of the most extraordinary of motoring history.

Britishers would also make the first east-west run across Africa by automobile, but it would be two young Americans, James Wilson and Francis Flood of Lincoln, Nebraska, who would conquer the Dark Continent by motorcycle.

Back in America in 1926, a transcontinental automobile trip may not have been high adventure, but it was still a sufficiently uncomfortable enterprise to cause most cross-country travelers to take the train. Automobiles were not air-conditioned, many were not heated, few had radios. Touring cars were open; side curtains could be buttoned down in the event of dust or rain, but no mistake about it, the motorists knew they were engaged in an outdoor sport. Such conditions, except in the name of adventure, were intolerable to most of the people who had reason to travel across the continent. Still, a long train trip could get boring. In 1926, for those who felt they needed a break in the trip, the great Southwest now offered a motorized diversion called the Indian Detours.

. . . On the Screen

In Sky High, *a 1922 film, Tom Mix is on the trail of some men who are smuggling Chinese across the Mexican border. Besides the appearance of automobiles,* Sky High *was also one of the first westerns to feature the use of an airplane.*

The Museum of Modern Art/ Film Stills Archive

In 1928 Tom Mix came to the rescue of Caryl Lincoln (playing Diana Cody) in a film called Hello Cheyenne. *In this movie, two rival telephone crews race to be the first to make connections between Rawhide and Cheyenne. Tom was on hand to roll rocks, ride horses, and rescue lonely lady motorists.*

The Museum of Modern Art/ Film Stills Archive

Back in the days when the train meant long-distance travel, it was not uncommon for passenger trains to run in several "sections" when the demand was great. All the sections ran on the same schedule, one following behind the other as close as was safely possible. Here, seven sections of Santa Fe Railway's California Limited *are about to depart Los Angeles; en route to Chicago, some of the passengers will likely detrain in New Mexico for a side trip on the Santa Fe's Indian Detours. Below, two Indian Detours cars climb over Cumbres Pass, elevation 10,003 feet. The pass lies between Chama, New Mexico, and Antonito, Colorado. A wonderful ride on a vintage narrow-gauge train can be taken through this same area today, on the Cumbres and Toltec Scenic Railroad.* **Above, Santa Fe Railway; below, Edward Kemp, Museum of New Mexico Collection**

6

Along the Detours Trail

T WAS ONE OF THOSE summer days in Arizona when the earth looked as if it would boil if given half a chance. Heat waves rolled off the dry land of the Indian reservation. The tourists' car sat at the edge of the road, a tire flat, the driver unable to get clearance under the axle for the jack. When he dug a hole for the jack, it wouldn't lift the wheel high enough to allow him to remove the wheel. Impasse. A dude from the Midwest, he didn't know anything about the desert. They had brought no water. No cars had appeared from either direction during the two hours they had been there. Sitting on the running board, looking up and down the road, staring out across the great silence, they were scared.

They saw the car before they heard it, its brightwork glinting at the base of a low dust plume as it rolled out of the east. The tourists jumped up and waved and the sedan rumbled to a stop behind theirs. The young driver, dressed in ten gallon hat, riding breeches and brown riding boots, introduced himself as Norbert Staab, of Santa Fe, a chauffeur for the Indian Detours. He was, he explained, carrying four tourists on a trip through the Navajo and Hopi country. He offered to help them change the flat tire.

While Staab's tourists and the woman guide, also an employee of the Indian Detours, shared their water with the parched Midwesterners, Staab searched around until he found a flat rock. He slid the rock in front of the flat tire, drove the car onto the rock, and placed the jack under the axle. The flat tire was changed in a matter of minutes. Good deed and desert survival lesson rendered, the likeable young fellow tipped his cowboy hat and rolled his Indian Detours car on into the west . . .

The Indian Detours?

The first official run of the Indian Detours hit the trail on the 15th of May, 1926, when a loaded Packard Eight touring car pulled away from the Castañeda Hotel, a Harvey House in Las Vegas, New Mexico. The car carried its precious cargo of tourists to La Fonda Hotel in Santa Fe by way of the Glorieta Pass, delivered them safely, and so one of the most unusual, and certainly the most ambitious of auto touring businesses in the history of American motoring got off to a successful start. That Packard Eight broke the trail for thousands of tourists who would travel millions of miles through the Southwest.

Few Americans—and even relatively few citizens of the modern Southwest—know very much at all about the Indian Detours, which always had its headquarters in Santa Fe and operated under the aegis of the Santa Fe Railway and its affiliated Fred Harvey business. The Indian Detours opened up the last dark corners of the Southwest. Its cultural and economic influence on the region is incalculable, its story one of adventure and romance. The Detours came along at just the right time. And in the right place.

Prior to the advent of the Indian Detours, long-distance train travelers had little or no opportunity to "get off the beaten track" for a side trip. After all, the roads were in such deplorable condition, why would anyone want to leave behind the comforts of the train? The folks in this photo, circa 1900, did the next best thing, apparently taking a private train along so as to travel in "civilized" manner through the vast, arid Southwest.
Santa Fe Railway

Major R. Hunter Clarkson, a war-decorated British cavalryman, was in charge of transportation at the Grand Canyon for the Harvey people. A railroad spur had been built to the Grand Canyon, the first train reaching there in September of 1901. Motor tours along the rim of the canyon were rolling soon after that and were still quite popular in the 1920s when Clarkson was in charge. It was Major Clarkson's felicitous notion that motor tours across the rest of the still untrammeled, beautiful Southwest should be a jolly fine adventure.

The Harvey House management, envisioning hotel rooms filled with those adventure-bound tourists, thought so too; and the boys down at the Santa Fe Railway, seeing full railway coaches in their collective mind's eye, agreed to the risk. Those were heady times, the 1920s; men were not afraid to take bold financial risks. After all, any fool could see that prosperity would last forever.

Motoring across the United States was still not a commonplace experience, coast-to-coast traffic staying on the trains, for the most part. Generally speaking, the people who could afford such travel did not have to drive a car if they didn't want to, and most didn't, so far as the western states were concerned.

But there did exist adventurous types among the train travelers who wanted to see more of the Southwest than they could see from a train window, or at railway stations such as at Albuquerque, where Indians would dance on cue on railway platforms and offer clay pots and other handmade curios for sale. Then the Indians would disappear until the next train was due. They may have known the train schedules better than the station masters. In any event, many of the travelers expressed an interest in seeing the "real thing," and an auto-touring company did exist already, the Koshare Tours, a precursor of the Indian Detours.

The Koshare Tours is forgotten now, remembered only in some yellowing brochures and the memories of a few older citizens who have lived in Albuquerque since the 1920s. Erna Fergusson and Ethel Hickey founded the Koshare Tours in about 1921 and operated the business until 1925, the year before the Indian Detours started operating. The Koshare Tours worked with the Santa Fe Railway, but there is no indication that the business was owned, even in part, by the railroad.

The Santa Fe Hotel and Fred Harvey Lunchroom at Belen, New Mexico.
Santa Fe Railway

The Santa Fe's California Limited, *apparently running in two or more sections, has stopped at Barstow, in California's Mojave Desert, circa 1926. The train is en route to Los Angeles. To the right stands the majestic* Casa Del Desierto *(House of the Desert), home of the Fred Harvey Hotel and Lunchroom in Barstow.*
Santa Fe Railway

the Indian-detour

Newest way to see oldest America on your Santa Fe - Fred Harvey way to and from California ◆

Three days personally-conducted motor tour in luxurious Harveycars through a region rich in history and mystery—the Enchanted Empire. Only $45 extra with everything provided—meals, lodging and motor transportation.

Westbound passengers leave trains at Las Vegas, New Mex., and join them again at Albuquerque, New Mex., three days later. Eastbound is just the reverse. This unusual tour comprises visits to old Santa Fe, also the inhabited Indian Pueblos of Tesuque, Santa Clara, San Juan, Santo Domingo and other places in the Upper Rio Grande Valley, as well as the huge ruin of Puyé a cliff pueblo twenty centuries old.

There will be optional side trips and "land cruises" in charge of specially trained couriers for those who wish to extend their travels off-the-beaten-path.

This service will begin May 15, 1926.

➤ mail this coupon

Mr. W. J. Black, Pass. Traf. Mgr., Santa Fe System Lines
No. 1101-A Railway Exchange, Chicago, Ill.

Am planning a trip to..this summer and would be glad to receive detailed information

about the Indian detour. There will be...persons in party.

Name...

Address...

Opposite, this ad appeared in the National Geographic *magazine prior to the inauguration of the Indian Detours. Above, the* California Limited *streaks through the Mojave Desert headed for Barstow and ultimately Chicago.* **Opposite, John Signor Collection; above, Santa Fe Railway**

The Koshare Tours used the air-cooled Franklin car, certainly not an inexpensive car, so the business must have been backed with a little money. It is known that Erna Fergusson was a member of a prominent New Mexico family. The Tours covered most of New Mexico, which surprises many people today, people who cannot imagine such extensive travel on a regular basis that long ago. Tours were run from Albuquerque as far south as Carlsbad Caverns and all the way up to Taos and the Red River area. A tour could even be organized to carry a traveler to the Grand Canyon, the Painted Desert and the Petrified Forest.

The Koshare company lasted for four years, so it must have been something of a success, but there seems to be no hard information as to why it folded. However, Erna Fergusson was hired by the Indian Detours in 1926 at a high salary and a substantial bonus to be their Chief Courier, that is, in charge of the women guides. Report-

edly she was a severe taskmaster. For whatever reason, she was replaced about 1929.

The headquarters of the Indian Detours was on Water Street, just south and across the street from La Fonda Hotel. The headquarters building is now a dry cleaning establishment, and the Detours garage, on the other corner just west of the Detours offices, is now a small downtown mall with a tourist shop in every corner. The Detours had a sales office in La Fonda Hotel also, and a hand-carved, painted Detours sign dating from the 1920s can be seen hanging in the lobby. Most modern travelers, if they notice the sign at all, must wonder what it represents.

With the backing of the Santa Fe and Fred Harvey, the Indian Detours certainly did not have to bootstrap its way to success. When the Detours hit the trail in May of 1926, it did so in brand new Packard Eight touring cars and several small White buses. The De-

Albuquerque Depot and the Alvarado Hotel

Albuquerque Depot and the Alvarado Hotel

The views on these two pages show the famous Alvarado Hotel complex located at Albuquerque, New Mexico. Opposite, above, is an overview of the depot (far left) and hotel circa 1905. In later years the tracks were elevated through the station to eliminate grade crossings, and the tower on the depot was shortened, opposite, below. The view directly above shows the entrance to the Fred Harvey Indian Building; behind it the Alvarado Hotel spreads out imposingly. At right, the entrance to the Indian Building as it appeared in later years. The Santa Fe/Fred Harvey hotel and depot complex served as a beginning or end point for some of the Indian Detour trips.

All, Santa Fe Railway

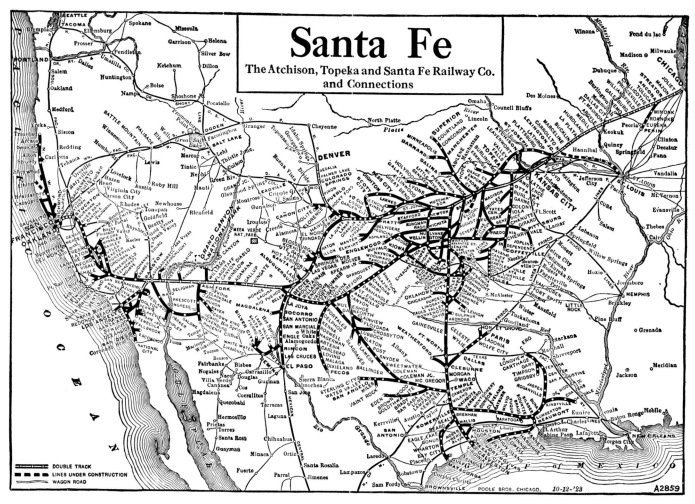

Santa Fe
The Atchison, Topeka and Santa Fe Railway Co. and Connections

POOLE BROS. CHICAGO. 10-12-'23 A2859

DOUBLE TRACK
LINES UNDER CONSTRUCTION
WAGON ROAD

A map of the Santa Fe Railway, circa 1925.

John Signor Collection

A Harvey car (at right) pulls away from La Fonda Hotel in downtown Santa Fe, New Mexico.
Margaret Wennips Moses Collection

tours was a class operation all the way down the line, from manager to mechanic, and no expense was spared to make it so.

Major Clarkson settled on the Packard Eight touring car after studying what machines were available. The Packard Eight was an imposing automobile with leather upholstery, a second windshield for rear seat passengers, and jump seats; it was officially classified as a seven-passenger car. The power plant was a big straight-eight engine. The Packard company soon advertised the fact that its machines were being used for "deluxe exploration" in the Southwest. The buses ordered came with swivel seats so that the passengers could swing around and not miss a thing.

The drivers were chosen carefully and just as carefully trained. They were local boys, and indeed they had to be, considering that most of the roads lacked direction or warning signs. It's not remembered who designed their boots-and-breeches outfits, which made them look rather like polo players inspired by Tom Mix. The men were excellent drivers, capable of taming the wildest cars in the west. During millions of Detours miles through the Southwest, not a single tourist was killed or seriously injured. In fact, the only Detours fatality was a driver who rolled his touring car when he lost control in deep gravel near Pilar, New Mexico.

The drivers were not allowed to drink, smoke, or chew tobacco in the presence of the dudes, and if a female passenger seemed to be paying more attention to him than to the scenery, he was not expected to return the compliment. Eyes and mind on the road, hands on the steering wheel and the gear shift lever *only* was the "advice" from the front office. Legend has it that the Santa Fe Railway was not beyond sending out a company-hired vamp to try to entice the boys beyond endurance. "They'd just throw themselves at you," a driver recalled years later, a nostalgic light in his eye. The men were expected to be strong, silent, capable . . . and stoic.

The drivers had to make minor repairs in the field. The cars carried planks attached under the running boards by wing nuts and tarps to help get the cars out of mud or sand, but they also carried—besides the inevitable shovel—a tool packet, spark plugs, distributor and fan belt, and at least one extra inner tube. Roadside repairs were often necessary; traffic was sparse and telephones few and *far* between.

The family of one driver still has the distributor the man repaired many years ago. When a part broke, he sat down by the side of the road and carved a splint for it out of a piece of wood. Such men inspired confidence in dudes from places like New York, Boston, and Philadelphia.

"You know," Norbert Staab said one day, the disbelief still evident in his voice over fifty years after the event, "I once met a woman from Philadelphia who had never seen a rainbow. Can you imagine that? Well, she saw one with me, a beautiful double rainbow up by Taos. Maybe it was worth the wait and the long trip."

The tourists were officially classifed as "detourists" by the Indian Detours management. It was the irreverent drivers who called them dudes, and dudes they remained until the end of Detours history. But if the drivers inspired confidence in the dudes, the couriers did also. If a mere slip of a girl will risk the wilderness on a daily basis, the tourists might have mused, it should be safe enough for me. It was. The couriers assured the tourists that neither Indians nor bandidos were likely to attack the car somewhere west of Santa Fe.

A Detours driver-mechanic rests on the bumper with one of the local residents at Taos Pueblo in the late 1920s. The cars are Packard Eights, mainstay of the Detours fleet from 1926 to 1929. **Alan Shules, Museum of New Mexico Collection**

If the drivers were to remain silent, for the most part, the tourists had the couriers along to fill their ears with information about the history of the land, the geology of the region, ethnology, art, archeology, and the flora and fauna spied alongside the road. "And," added Courier Margaret Wennips Moses years later, "almost any other -ology you can think of."

It has been generally forgotten that the couriers were in charge of the tours. They made the decisions about when and where to go. They chattered on at high speed about everything in sight as the Harveycar rolled through the scenery. They wet-nursed the dudes, even to the extent of getting up early to make sure a lunch would be ready for them. The couriers perched on one of the jump seats just in front of the dudes where they could communicate with the driver or the tourists with equal facility, and be ready to short circuit any tall tales the drivers might be inclined to pass on as gospel. The boys could tell some dillies, an ex-courier recalled.

Many of the couriers became capable survivalists. One bright morning along about 1931 a Detours Cadillac broke a spring in the canyon on the way to Taos. The chauffeur, a new man, got down to inspect his suddenly listing machine. After a brief deliberation, he shook his head and announced to his anxious passengers that they would have to stay right there until help came up the road. The tourists looked worriedly at the indifferent cliffs above them and at the tumbling Rio Grande just over the edge of the road. The place was lonely, frightening.

The courier on the trip was Lucille Stacy (née Ridout) and she was *not* new at her job. "After suggesting that help might be a long time coming," she said, "I got down

Three views of Indian Detours couriers and the uniforms they wore. Left, Margaret Wennips is perched on the bumper of a Detours Packard sedan, probably in the canyon of the Rio Grande on the way to Taos. Below, left, (thought to be) courier Winifred Shuler rises to the occasion and helps driver Frank Carroon dig a Cadillac out of the mud. Below, Helen Davies of Santa Fe, in 1982, wearing the same outfit and Indian jewelry she wore when she was a courier in the 1930s. **Left, Margaret Wennips; below, left, Museum of New Mexico; below, Albert Manchester**

to see what could be done to get us rolling again. It was easy enough to fix. We found a driftwood log down by the river, wedged it in under the car body, and wired it in place. Then we headed for Taos, where I hoped we could get the thing repaired."

No repairs were found in Taos. A new Cadillac spring for that particular model was unavailable, and the blacksmiths and mechanics in town told Lucille that's what the car needed. The jury-rig she had figured out was as good as anything Taos had to offer, and so the touring car limped stiffly back to Santa Fe.

"And *I* was bawled out for getting back late," Lucille recalled. "Better late than never, I say. We could have been there still. In those days you had to be prepared to help yourself."

Lucille Stacy was a courier for twelve years and during that time she did not lose a single dude. Most of the couriers, she pointed out, were from the West, and probably more capable and independent than most young women of the time. When in her seventies, she herself built the adobe house she lived in for the last few years of her life, her two sons helping her with the roof and the cabinets.

The couriers were well educated, mostly college graduates. Lucille Stacy had studied anthropology, botany and geology; she could read the land and she knew the cultures of the Southwest. She was on a dig at Puyé when she caught sight of her first Indian Detours car, which pulled up below the escarpment and disgorged a group of tourists and the courier. Lucille watched as the Kodak-toting dudes risked the rickety ladders while their courier answered some extraordinarily unlikely questions ("Why did the Indians build the pueblos and make their caves so far from the railroads?") with simple, good answers, never patronizing the tourists. Lucille was fascinated. The very next time she was in Santa Fe she went down to the Indian Detours office to inquire whether a young woman with her qualifications might not be able to become a courier.

She found out that she was exactly what the Detours was looking for. She discovered, too, that she would be expected to return to classes with the rest of the couriers, who all continued to study various aspects of the Southwestern scene with recognized authorities such as instructors from the University of New Mexico. They studied in classrooms and in the field—at Indian ruins,

The garage for the Indian Detours cars and buses. This location is in Santa Fe, just across Water Street from La Fonda Hotel. The building looks much the same today, but is now a small downtown mall full of tourist shops. **Dorothy Raper Miller Collection**

A group of Harveycar driver-mechanics standing tall in front of La Fonda Hotel, circa 1929.

in Spanish mountain villages, and in modern Indian pueblos. Absolutely nothing was left to chance with the Indian Detours, whether it was the drivers, the couriers, or the cars. Lucille soon learned, however, that there was danger in knowing too much. A naturally shy woman, it was just possible that she tried to hide her shyness behind a smoke screen of erudition.

"At first I answered questions with textbook answers," she said, "and I even used Latin names for plants we spotted along the road. Nobody knew what I was talking about. I left the dudes rolling their eyes with bewilderment or laughing at the notion that one small woman could know so much. I managed to simplify my delivery."

At least one of the couriers had been a dude; Helen Davies, of Santa Fe, first rode in an Indian Detours car in 1927 when she traveled through the Southwest with her mother and sister. She recalls that the driver and the courier became lost and the car arrived at its destination quite late that night. "A trail then was a wagon trail," she said, "and very often we steered by landmarks, just as the pioneers had." Helen had read a lot of Zane Grey's works and she credits this casual study with some of her success as a courier. Unlike most of the couriers, she was not a Westerner.

Bulletins were issued occasionally to keep pace with the questions the imaginative dudes would pose, and the couriers were expected to keep a notebook for these. Almost fifty years after starting her notebook, Rita Staab, Norbert Staab's wife, still had hers. In it a young courier could find an answer to some of the most bizarre questions a tourist might think to ask about the South-

west. But however bizarre the questions might seem to a Westerner (to this day many Easterners still think New Mexico is a foreign country), the courier and driver were supposed to maintain their composure. Major Clarkson was known to send "spy dudes" out on the trail just to test the couriers. The detourist was an honored guest; he or she would not be insulted by an impatient Detours employee.

The couriers too had their distinctive uniform. After some trial and error, an attractive outfit was fashioned, practical as well as pleasing to the eye. The Navajo style blouses were of various brilliant colors, and were of either velveteen or corduroy. A simple skirt was generally worn, although boots and jodphurs were sometimes substituted for rough country or climbing among Indian ruins. All of the women wore silver and turquoise jewelry—squash blossom necklaces, bracelets, and flashing concho belts. Lucille Stacy traded her old car for a concho belt. On their wide-brimmed, soft "outing hats" they carried the thunderbird emblem of the Indian Detours.

* * *

STEEP, ROUGH mountain roads, sand, mud and desert heat meant plenty of maintenance and preventive maintenance for the Harveycar fleet. Again, nothing was left to chance to make these high-toned safaris a success. Major Clarkson's by-the-book military mind contrived a maintenance program that was so thorough it was later adopted by some local governmental agencies.

Maintenance started with the drivers. A "Trip Re-

port" was completed when a car was returned to the garage after a trip. In-and-out odometer readings were noted and total mileage computed. Any gas and oil purchases were recorded, and tire changes were marked down so that the history could be kept of each Goodyear Double Eagle, the tire the Detours cars rolled on.

Other items checked off after each trip were in reference to the engine, clutch, transmission, differential, brakes, Bijur system, steering gear, dash instruments, wheels, body, chains, tools, and any unusual noises heard or located. The incoming driver was responsible for topping off the gasoline, and for checking the oil and topping that off too, if need be. Finally, he checked tire pressure on every wheel, including the spares. Failure to follow company procedure was tantamount to immediate dismissal. All of this attention to detail was simply to ensure the safety and comfort of the dudes.

After all of the machine's vital fluids had been replenished and its mechanical health checked out, the car was turned over to a "swamper," who swept out the car, washed it, and then polished its brightwork. Major Clarkson was known to inspect the cars personally, so when the car was deemed ready for one of his surprise inspections, it was lined up with the others in the dark garage, with regimental precision, standing clean and shiny.

The next driver to take the car out checked everything *again*. But in spite of all this attention to detail and the meticulous maintenance, the careful records kept on each car led to some painful discoveries; the big Packards seemed to be wearing out when they had clocked only about 30,000 miles. More maintenance and the periodic inspection of parts did not seem to help. The Packards may have been the "acme of comfort

and luxury in transportation," as one of their 1928 ads said, and riding in one of them may have been right next door to riding on a Santa Fe Pullman car, but as far as surviving in the Southwest was concerned, they didn't have what it takes. One of the ex-drivers recalled that their main faults lay in their greasing and oiling systems; the Packards just didn't stand up to daily workouts in sand and dust.

Major Clarkson looked over the rest of the automotive field and he settled on the Cadillac, ordering

Standing beside a 1929 Cadillac 341-B, an Indian Detours courier lectures two hardy dudes during a winter tour. **Museum of New Mexico**

1929 open and closed models, the touring cars the 341-B. These cars became the mainstay of the Indian Detours as the Packards were phased out. They proved to be rugged and dependable, comfortable and roomy, and their big V-8 engines provided plenty of smooth power for the wild country they had to traverse. The closed cars even had heaters, something of an improvement over the lap robes used in the Packards. The high altitude country of northern New Mexico can get downright chilly, as a lot of dudes discovered.

The Indian Detours proved to be an immediate, unqualified success. With Americans in a traveling mood, and with a large enough middle class to fill the Harveycars and the small buses, the Indian Detours became one of the most popular diversions ever invented for cross-country train travelers. The roads of the Southwest weren't that good, but they were at least passable, most of the time. The cars were good enough, possibly uncomfortable by today's standards, but if you wanted to see the great American outback in the late 1920s, a ride in a Cadillac was about as much comfort as you could expect.

It's ironical that the Atchison, Topeka and the Santa Fe did not pass through Santa Fe, but it's a fact. Passengers for Santa Fe descended from the train at Lamy, a small town about twenty miles south of Santa Fe, where the Detours cars and buses picked them up. From there, the train went on to Albuquerque. The travelers, now detourists, were taken to La Fonda Hotel on the southeast corner of the plaza in Santa Fe, one of the monuments of Santa Fe and still very much the center of town.

A simple one-day tour of Santa Fe—*A Day in old Santa Fe*—could be arranged, or one could go farther afield. For example, a dude might choose tour number six, a two-day excursion to Taos . . .

After the dudes had breakfasted at La Fonda, they would find the Harveycar waiting for them outside the hotel at 8:45. Generally speaking, no more than four tourists would be taken in a Harveycar. Their luggage for the short trip would be packed on the car. A lunch would have been put up for them by the Harveygirls and the leather lunch box would be loaded onto the car. The driver carried water up front with him, and, if a gentleman had thought about the "problem" and had slipped the driver a few dollars, a thermos of bourbon could be on board too, in spite of Prohibition. The courier saw to it that everybody and everything got into or onto the car.

(Please note here that the Indian Detours couriers were *not* Harveygirls, who were in fact the young women who worked as waitresses in the Harvey hotels and railroad depot restaurants. There were many Harveygirls, to the everlasting delight of cowboys and commercial travelers, but there were very few *couriers*, the young women who guided the Indian Detours excursions.)

And so we're off . . .

The big rumbling tourer climbs the hill north of town. The sky is wonderfully clear; summer rains do not usually arrive until the afternoon. The morning air at seven thousand feet is bracing. The smoky-green Sangre de Cristo Mountains rise to the right, a hint of snow remaining on them even in early summer. The Jemez Mountains, farther away, rise to the west. After a few days on the train, the relative freedom of the automobile is exhilarating. Although old, settled almost as long ago as any other place in America, New Mexico looks clean, fresh.

They roll by Black Mesa, a conspicuous volcanic butte that guards the southern end of the Española Valley. The courier advises the dudes that the butte is called *Tunyo* by the Indians and is a place of mythology for them, as well as one of the last refuges from the sword-wielding, cross-bearing Spaniards. But the *conquistadores* did eventually overwhelm the Indians on their seemingly impregnable aerie. The Pueblo Indians were, after all, relatively peaceful agrarians; the Spanish had been practicing warfare with the Moors for centuries. The dudes nod, wondering why they had never before heard any of this exciting history.

The driver pushes on to San Ildefonso, a pueblo of Tewa-speaking Indians. Here in an Indian village, surrounded by real live Indians, the trip starts to get darned interesting. The Indian women bring out clay pots for the tourists to examine. San Ildefonso was the home of Maria Martinez, who fashioned exquisite black pottery. But her pots weren't "colorful," possibly not what the tourists had expected. But those tourists who

coughed up the few dollars she was asking at the time were extremely lucky; today, her pottery is cherished by collectors and museums.

Up a canyon then and across the plateau to Puyé. Ruins and cliff dwellings extend for about a mile along the escarpment. Ruins cluster on top of the mesa, too, and the dudes learn that the Indians most probably lived up there during the summer to catch the breezes, then moved over the side of the south-facing cliff to bask in the sun during the winter months. Damned clever of them, the dudes decide as they scramble over ruins and up and down ladders, the courier warning them to *please* be careful. Some of the dudes, certainly not all, climb ladders right to the top. The rest poke around below, pocketing a few pottery sherds that litter the slopes and still turn up every spring and after every heavy rain.

The dudes with the right stuff discover that the view from the top of the mesa is worth the risk of the climb. The Española Valley and Black Mesa lie below and to the east, and beyond that the land rises to the Sangre de Cristo Mountains. The dudes listen to the wind sighing through the piñons. A raven floats by at eye level. The tourists might be struck by the loneliness of the place, hit between the eyes by infinity, maybe just a bit depressed by notions of the transitoriness of life and civilizations. In spite of the scary ladder—worse going down than up, they discover—they are glad to descend to the car and their warm, affable companions; and possibly to a first sampling of that bourbon, which, surprisingly, turns out to be the real thing.

Some miles up the road the driver wheels the big car onto the plaza at Santa Clara Pueblo. The dust hasn't had a chance to settle before the Indian women are emerging with their *ollas* and *tinajas*, more black pottery of beautiful design. And if this just happens to be a feast day, the dudes might just get a chance to see and photograph a ritual dance (edited to protect religious secrets). This is it, boy, no cigar store Indians here!

Across the Rio Grande again at Española and up the winding, deep canyon, climbing toward Taos. The courier now explains that they had dropped two thousand feet after leaving Santa Fe and now they will regain the altitude. The dudes look up apprehensively at boulders clinging above them while the driver skirts others that have already fallen into the road. Climbing out of the canyon at last, they are treated to another portion of it, to their left, which looks for all the world like part of the Grand Canyon. After a long day filled with new sights and sensations, the dudes bounce into Taos, a quaint mud town resting on the high plains between the Rio Grande and the Sangre de Cristo Mountains. They get down from the car in the dusty plaza, where they jostle with the cowboys, farmers and blanket-wrapped Indians. Horse-drawn wagons are tied up in the plaza alongside dirty flivvers. After dinner at their approved stop, the Don Fernando Hotel, some of the dudes, the smart ones, tumble into bed. The livelier tourists decide to see what's happening over at Long John Dunn's gambling den.

The next morning the Indian Detours car rolls into

Taos Pueblo, that *piece de resistance* in the matter of Indian pueblos. A multi-storied adobe complex rises on each side of a cold mountain stream. The courier is in her glory here, carrying on at great length while the driver chats with Indian friends he hasn't seen since his last run to Taos. The men sit on the car bumper, rolling cigarettes, talking about the weather, crops, the dudes, watching the dudes line up to get their photo snapped in front of the oldest inhabited dwelling in the United States. And it sure looks like it.

They unlimber their Kodaks and snap away, themselves in the foreground, a few blanket-wrapped Indians and the pueblo buildings behind them, the sacred mountain for a backdrop.

After the pueblo, and if the dudes are interested, the driver could take them by a few artists' studios. Taos, the dudes learn, has been an art colony for many years, the artists drawn by the colorful surroundings, the clear air and sky. Then it's off for Santa Fe.

But the tour has by no means ended.

On the way back to Santa Fe they pull up a ridge to Truchas, a Spanish village clinging to the mountain on both sides of the road. Shy faces and woolly heads are just visible through doorways and windows. Women in black, shawls over their heads, hurry along the road. Chickens squawk and dash back and forth in front of the car. If any of the tourists has been to mountain villages in Spain, those ancient places that cling to the top of hills, streets just wide enough to allow the passage of a man on horseback, then in Truchas he or she must feel a surge of *dejà vu*. In Truchas the dudes are on the mountains they could see from the ruins on top of the mesa at Puyé. Higher mountains are very close to the east. A cool wind, carrying with it a breath of the past winter, flows down from above. The Española Valley is far below and to the west.

Back down the ridge, the driver turns left onto another road. They drive into the crowded village of Cor-

This is the cover from a beautiful 70-page brochure the Indian Detours put out in 1929. The artist appears to have been an F. Seary.
R. Houchin Collection

Taking the *Indian Detour*

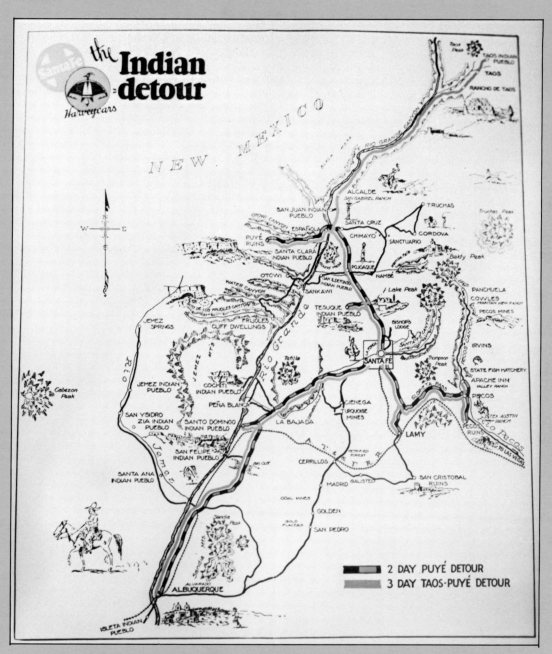

This map shows the trips a dude could hope to make. From the 1929 brochure. **R. Houchin Collection**

Above, a Harveycoach pauses in front of San Miguel Mission in Santa Fe. Travelers could pause from their cross-country train trip for a one-day tour of the old Spanish capital. Right, this is the La Fonda Hotel as it appeared in the late 1920s; two Harveycoaches wait outside for dudes on an early summer morning. From the 1929 brochure.

Above, Dorothy Raper Miller Collection; right, R. Houchin Collection

A pause on the Detours trail. The courier, Margaret Wennips, is sitting on the runningboard of the Cadillac sedan, studying something through binoculars. The dudes were from Colorado, two sisters and a brother.

Margaret Wennips Moses Collection

Dudes were wearing plus fours at this obvious tourist attraction, an "old Indian-Spanish-American Well," located at Glorieta, between Las Vegas, New Mexico, and Santa Fe. Left, courier Margaret Wennips Moses serving a picnic lunch along the Detours trail.

Both, Margaret Wennips Moses Collection

Some dudes resting along the Detours trail, enjoying a picnic lunch in the shade while sitting on the runningboard of a 1930 Cadillac. Below, somewhere on the Santa Fe Trail, east of Santa Fe. From the 1929 brochure.

Above, Margaret Wennips Moses Collection; below, R. Houchin Collection

A Harveycar and Harveycoach wait by the ancient Pecos Mission. The Sangre de Cristo Mountains rise in the background. From the 1929 brochure. Below, dudes munching on sandwiches in the wilds of New Mexico. A Harvey picnic box went out on many of the runs. **Above, R. Houchin Collection; below, Margaret Wennips Moses Collection**

Two couriers introduce a group of dudes to some Indian children at San Ildefonso Pueblo, northwest of Santa Fe. The Harveycoach driver looks on from beside his vehicle.
Museum of New Mexico

Taking the Indian Detour

A Harveycar and Harveycoach at the Puye Cliff Dwellings north of Santa Fe. This was an easy ride from Santa Fe, a popular trip for the dudes. From the 1929 brochure. Below, a Harveycar and Harveycoach at an Indian Pueblo, circa 1930.
Above, R. Houchin Collection; below, Margaret Wennips Moses Collection

A Harveycar stands in front of the oldest inhabited dwelling in the U.S., Taos Pueblo. From the 1929 brochure. Below, courier Margaret Wennips Moses, on left, with a couple of dudes and an old friend somewhere along the Detours trail.
Above, R. Houchin Collection; below, Margaret Wennips Moses Collection

Taking the **Indian Detour**

A 1930 Cadillac sedan at Quarai, New Mexico, the ruins of a Spanish mission built around 1630 and abandoned in about 1674 because of pressure from the Apaches. The Indian Detours would carry a tourist wherever he wanted to go, for weeks at a time if so desired. Below, Margaret Wennips out of uniform. She is second from right, in foreground, guiding a few dudes through the Canyon de Chelly. Trips can be taken today through the canyon in open cars; it is a memorable trip.

CHIEF OF THE SUN WORSHIPERS-   Pen drawing from Painting by E.I.Couse, N·A.

the Indian-detour

The America of Coronado waits for you beside this motor trail

An enchanted land, where for three days your luxurious Harveycar carries you on a personally-escorted motor tour of ancient Indian pueblos and prehistoric cliff-dwellings in the New Mexico Rockies between Las Vegas, Santa Fé and Albuquerque.

A new motor link in the Santa Fe cross-continent rail journey to and from California. Only $50 with everything provided—meals, lodging with bath every night and motor transportation.

On the Indian-detour you are still the guest of Santa Fe-Fred Harvey in every detail of accommodation and fine service. Ask for picture folder.

mail this ➤

W. J. Black, Pass. Traf. Mgr., Santa Fe System Lines
1142A Railway Exchange, Chicago, Ill.
   Please send me free picture folder about the Indian-detour.

....

....

Another Indian Detours ad from National Geographic, *probably in the late 1920s; by this time, the price for the tours had risen somewhat.*
John Signor Collection

dova, the home of many talented wood-carvers. After Cordova, the tour continues down the ridge and rolls into Chimayó, which with its *santuario* is a place of pilgrimage for Catholics from all over the Southwest and Mexico. The adobe chapel, built in the early 1880s, waits out eternity surrounded by giant cottonwoods. The religious art inside is crude yet moving, especially the large *retablo*. A stream gurgles by the front of the chapel, the warm breeze stirs the cottonwood leaves.

Chimayó is a restful place, a place the tourists might like to linger for at least a brief time. (Years later many New Mexican National Guardsmen will be captured on Bataan. They pledge that the survivors will hang their dog tags in the chapel once they get back to New Mexico. A passing visitor, seeing those dog tags today, may well wonder why they are all hanging there in a bunch.) But it's time to go, climb into the now familiar car, drive back to Santa Fe, the hotel . . . the twentieth century.

* * *

Most of the dudes who experienced a "motorcruise" in a Harveycar would have agreed that they had had a wonderful forty-five dollar adventure. The trip had proved to be safe enough, the driver a competent gentleman, the courier lively and informative. Many of the tourists saw things and places they had not known existed in their country. Indeed, too many of them did not know that New Mexico was a state. Some had worried about passports, visas, the rate of exchange, the language. Most dudes found a ride with the Detours through some of the darker corners of the Southwest exciting and educational, even entertaining. A few returned year after year. Norbert Staab told about two women from Philadelphia who would come every year and hire him, without a courier, to drive them for weeks at a time through the Indian country, the women sleeping in schoolhouses, he in the car. One delicate gentleman, a well known musical conductor, liked to come out to fish for trout. Since Norbert knew most of the good trout holes between Chama and Carlsbad, the old boy would hire him by the day for the fishing trips. Poor Norbert would have to carry the celebrated maestro piggyback from one side of the stream to the other, but Detours employees were not beyond giving a little extraordinary service.

The couriers and the drivers all agreed that, for whatever reason, the "best dudes" came in winter, spring and fall. The hardest to handle would always arrive in the summer. The best and the worst dudes came from New York, many intelligent, informed, a few the most dismal bores to penetrate west of the Pecos.

Some dudes didn't like the trips at all. They found the country too dry and empty for their taste, too lonely, cruel, the villages squalid and the people dirty. Such

This ad appeared in the February 1930 issue of Nature Magazine. *The Indian Detours trips were advertised in many publications; tickets for a Detours trip could even be purchased in Europe. Price for the trips was still on the upswing in this ad.*
Albert Manchester Collection

types were often the nouveau riche, the Detours employees thought. Many of the famous and wealthy who risked a ride through the Wild West with the Detours proved to be the best sports.

By 1929 the Indian Detours cars were carrying dudes all over the Southwest, even to Death Valley in California. Besides Santa Fe, Harveycars could be hired in Albuquerque and Winslow, Arizona. It's difficult now to realize what an impact the Indian Detours had on the Southwest. The twentieth century rode into many parts of the country in a Harveycar, the entire Southwest suddenly opened up to people who were afraid to drive across one of our last frontiers by themselves.

Many of the old Detours trips can be followed today. Most of the roads are now paved, but other than that surprisingly little has changed. One recent traveler, comparing his photos with the pictures his father had snapped in the late 1920s, found frightening similarities. He said that he got the eery feeling he was living his father's life all over again.

Nineteen twenty-nine came and went. The Depression gathered momentum, although there was not much business in New Mexico and the other states of the Southwest to depress. But the dudes stopped coming in such numbers as they had before. A lot of them were staying home to watch the shop, if they still had a shop to watch.

The Detours were not quite the same after the midthirties, after the equipment started aging, after the folks who had to work for a living could no longer go on chauffeured, guided tours. By then the Detours was a lot more class than most Americans needed. If fun seemed to be the national destiny in the 1920s, survival replaced it in the 1930s.

At the same time, spurred by federal support to provide jobs, the national highway system improved. And cars were better. A fellow no longer feared packing his family into the car for a vacation drive out to the West Coast. The Indian Detours became an anachronism, finally put to rest with gasoline and tire rationing at the outbreak of World War II. Although there are lineal descendents of the Indian Detours, touring companies with cars and buses, none of them ever compared in style with the first six or seven years of the Indian Detours.

When the Indian Detours is remembered now, it is always the early days that are recalled . . . the natty dudes with their Kodaks and flasks, the chatty couriers, the chauffeurs dressed like characters out of a bad Hollywood western, and a big touring car rumbling down a dusty dirt road, all headed for a distant pass.

The bridge at Otowi, once used by Indian Detours vehicles. Built in the 1920s, it crosses the Rio Grande between Santa Fe and Los Alamos. A newer bridge is located about 200 feet north; the old bridge is unsafe for anything but foot traffic these days. Photo taken in 1981.
Albert Manchester

Our 1937 Ford at rest on a Canadian provincial road south of Dawson Creek, British Columbia. This road was slick and required some tricky wheel work if another vehicle was met coming from the opposite direction.
Albert Manchester

On the Alaska Highway at last—but out of gas. It was several hours before one of us could get back to the car with a can of gas. The side panels of the engine had been dismounted to fight fires. **Albert Manchester**

End of the Trails

ear Mom,
WE ARE HAVING a great time up here. Plenty of bumpy, muddy roads. We hope to get to Alaska pretty soon. The car is holding together and we are too."

This is from a card I posted to my mother from Canada on the 26th of May, 1951. I was seventeen, between junior and senior years in high school, and, with two high school buddies, off to spend the summer in Alaska. The car mentioned was a 1937 Ford V-8 60, which meant it had a 60 h.p. engine, or what was left of sixty horses after fourteen years. Most Fords built during this period came with 85 horses. We were underpowered. To compound our problem, our dainty car had a "high speed" rear end. Underpowered and overgeared, a terrible combination for wilderness driving. The car had cost us $85. We were not aware when we started that our car had been intended for the flatlands and for town driving, but by the time we got to Anchorage you can bet we knew it.

In two weeks in Canada and Alaska we ruined what had been a perfectly good car. Oh, it had some miles on it before we started, but there was nothing wrong with it. My buddies and I were pretty good mechanics. We'd gone through it. The Ford was OK. The problem was the roads.

In 1951, in the spring, just *getting* to the Alaska Highway could be the hardest part of your trip. The "spring breakup" in the North is not the end of a winter romance. Well, the Canadian provincial roads didn't break up so much as they *dissolved*. You could get right down there plowing mud with your front bumper. That deep. I mean you didn't need brakes. Just take your foot off the throttle, you'd stop dead. And lucky to get going again if you dared stop.

You couldn't take an "alternate route." Mostly they didn't exist, and if one did exist in was just as bad as the road you were on. Spring in Canada spelled MUD. The disintegration of our car began when the taillight lense fell off.

In 1951 the Alaska Highway had been open to civilian traffic for just a few years. The Canadian Traffic Control Board was still sensitive about naive Yanks who insisted on launching themselves and their machines into northern Canada on bad roads, and they insisted—rightly so—that one's automobile be in first class mechanical order and equipped with sufficient spare tires, tubes, tools, a gas can, and an overnight camping outfit. Mounties we met along the Highway— one of them picturesquely dressed in his red tunic— were, to say the least, surprised to meet three seventeen-year-olds from Minnesota cruising through that remote scenery in a fourteen-year-old car. Babes in the North Woods. Young fools rushing into the subarctic as fast as we dared go. Just where the devil did we think we were going? Alaska. Alaska, eh? Raised eyebrows. A once over of the muddy car. Think you can make it, boys? Sure. A nod. Okay, have a good time. And be careful.

Sympathetic men. We were lucky none of them saw us when we were putting out our occasional fires. The carb started to flood and we couldn't figure out why. The engine caught fire several times. As soon as we saw smoke, we would skid to a stop, leap out, and throw gravel and sand on the engine. If the road had been paved, we would have lost the car. We dismounted the side panels of the engine compartment to give us quick access to the fires. Our engine wiring became a mass of electricians tape. But nobody ever caught us as we leaped about throwing dirt at the car. There was no traffic. You could drive for hours and never see another vehicle. Stops for gasoline, repairs, or food between Dawson Creek, British Columbia, where the Alaska Highway starts, and Fairbanks, Alaska, about 1,600 miles away at that time, averaged over a hundred miles apart.

In 1942 that wilderness had been the scene of the most extraordinary activity as U.S. Army Engineers and thousands of civilians worked twenty-four hours a day, seven days a week to do what old-timers in Alaska said was impossible: build a road to Alaska during one summer.

But they HAD to do the job in one summer.

The Japanese were in the Aleutians and it was feared they might get a foothold in North America. The "miracle at Midway" did not occur until June of 1942. The Alaska Highway was built to open a supply route to Alaska, a route beyond the range of carrier-based airplanes. Contrary to the expectations of everybody but the U.S. Army Engineers, supply trucks were rumbling all the way to Alaska over the new road at the rate of about one every three minutes by the end of the year. The Alaska Highway went through as if the outcome of the war depended upon it, and in early 1942 there was nobody to say that wasn't the case.

The road to Alaska went through at an average of eight completed miles per day. Each company of engineers was assigned a twenty mile stretch to finish off, and when that section was completed, the company would leapfrog up the line and start over on another stretch of virgin wilderness. There were several "working points." Troops started at Dawson Creek, working north. Other troops were entrained at Skagway and sent to Whitehorse over the White Pass and Yukon Railway, and they worked north *and* south. Another regiment pushed south from Alaska.

The Alaska Highway is now shorter—*much* straightened and leveled—and good bridges have replaced the original structures, some of which still existed in 1951. That spring we came upon tractors, anchored to trees at the top of steep hills slippery with mud, winching trucks up the inclines. Bridges had washed away. Other tractors pulled vehicles across shallow rivers and streams. Our '37 Ford spun up the hills and bounced across the streams without any help from anybody. Foolhardy but fun, wiseacre kids, grinning and waving as we roared (we lost our muffler) and splashed past everybody.

It seems likely the Ford engineers had never intended the V-8 60 to be a wilderness trekker. Without our muffler we snarled viciously at the mountains, but we were much more bark than bite. The high speed rear end caused us to climb almost every hill in low gear. And, because we had mechanical brakes, we had to creep down every hill in low gear, the driver pushing on the brake pedal for all he was worth, the front passenger hauling back on the emergency brake while, at the same time, holding the gear shift in first gear. The transmission was a bit worn and it tended to jump out of gear when we were in long, steep descents.

Our windshield wiper didn't work well. A couple of windows cracked. The lights stopped working. The generator conked out. Or tried to. We tortured it back to life every fifty or a hundred miles by taking off the inspection plate and running a screwdriver over the armature until the thing started charging again. Brutal. But it worked. Better than waiting two weeks for another one to come up the highway. We drove through rain and snow. Tires blew. We fixed flats right in the middle of the road, pumping up the tires with a hand pump. Just like in the old days.

We rattled into Alaska one day when the sun was out and the sky the purest, cleanest arctic blue. The brown slash of the Alaska Highway stretched on through the forest, on into Alaska. We had made it. Many other adventures awaited us that summer, but the Alaska Highway part of it was behind us. The Ford survived just a few days in Anchorage. A piston broke. With no money left for repairs, we traded it off to a fellow who wanted the high-speed rear end. He paid us $150 for what was left of our V-8 60. No, there wasn't much left. Canada's provincial roads and the Alaska Highway had finished her. In two weeks.

* * *

1933 SEEMS TO BE a good place to end a story about the pioneer days of driving in the Far West, exactly thirty years after Dr. Jackson had pushed his 1903 Winton across the country. Nineteen thirty-three is a good year to choose because that's the year Franklin Roosevelt became president. After that, a good deal of federal money was spent on the national highway system, as much to give people a wage as to improve the roads. Many roads were paved during this period, although even in the 1940s many main highways in the West (I remember them) were still just graveled.

The idea for our classic highway, Route 66, was spawned in 1927, but complete construction and paving was not finished until 1937. The average cost of each mile of Route 66 was $22,000. A mile of a modern interstate can cost millions. Today, when you're driving west of Albuquerque on I-40, you can still catch glimpses of 66 where it angles off, crumbling, covered with sand, tumbleweed, and memories, toward distant mesas. Then, farther on, it angles back to you, runs under I-40, and meanders off in the other direction. Looking at 66, looking at where it goes, you get the feeling folks in the past pointed their roads at the scenery, whimsically, so nobody would miss anything of value.

But it must have been fairly easy to drive across the country to the West Coast by 1930. It must have been,

The Casa Blanca Auto Court in Salt Lake City, from a postcard James Aune picked up there in 1930. This is quite a modern layout for the time.
Albert Manchester Collection

James Bryan Aune and the car he drove all the way from Minnesota to California and back, in 1930. The car doesn't look too much the worse for wear, so it couldn't have been too hard a trip. **Albert Manchester Collection**

because my Uncle James Bryan Aune did it in that year. I have a collection of photographs he took on the trip, and a collection of postcards he gathered along the way. He passed through Colorado Springs. Photos of rocks. A bridge—"Part of the desert"—over an arroyo. James clowning, waving at the camera as he heads off toward an outhouse in a clump of trees. His wife Genevieve, dressed to the nines, standing at attention beside a road in Colorado. I have the camera he used to take the pictures, a Kodak No. 2 Folding Cartridge Premo. I'm sure James didn't go again. He wasn't a traveling man, so if he would drive all that way it must have been easy enough to get there. But maybe it was rough enough so that he decided once was enough. I should have asked him.

* * *

IF DRIVING ALMOST ANYPLACE one wished to go in the United States had become a more or less commonplace experience, travel across much of Africa was still extraordinary. We have mentioned briefly the adventures of Major and Mrs. Court Treatt who drove their Crossleys from Cape Town to Cairo, so it seems only nationalistically right we say something about the Flood-Wilson motorcycle expedition that crossed Africa, from Nigeria to the Red Sea, in 1931-1932.

Francis Flood and James Wilson were not the first to drive motor vehicles on the east-west axis across Africa. This distinction goes to some Britishers who drove a couple of Jowett automobiles across the continent in the late 1920s. The Jowett, by the way, was well known in its day as a totally reliable machine; the company did

not change the basic engine design for *forty years.*

Flood and Wilson, two zany Nebraskans in their late twenties, left the United States in 1931 on a trip around the world. They would pay for the adventures by writing newspaper articles. The dirty freighter they were on arrived at the sweltering west coast of Africa and then limped from port to port as it worked its way south. Cape Town was far away, and it looked like they were destined to nose into a lot of ugly towns before getting there. Not only was the trip tedious and uncomfortable, there wasn't a heck of a lot to write about. It occurred to them that it might be more exciting to cross the still relatively dark continent.

But how? No roads, no railroads existed in Central Africa. The French Citroen Expedition had penetrated that part of the continent, and the Jowetts had crossed just below the Sahara, but that was all the motor traffic that part of Africa had so far seen.

Then one day Flood and Wilson were bouncing along a trail in Nigeria on a borrowed Triumph motorcycle. The inspiration hit Wilson right between the eyes.

Motorcycles!

What a hell of a stunt it would be . . .

Two blue and gray Triumphs were located at a motorcycle agency in Lagos. The Triumph Cycle Company took a chance on the Yanks and furnished the machines for the adventure. (Hmmmmm. If those crazy Americans should live through the ghastly ordeal and get all the way across with our motorbikes, why there'll be no end of publicity.) The bikes, weighing only three hundred pounds, were one-lungers with three-speed transmissions. Sidecars were mounted to carry food, extra gas, spare parts, tools, and personal gear, which included a banjo.

The Flood-Wilson Trans-Africa Motorcycle Expedi-

tion sallied from Lagos, Nigeria, on November 10, 1931. Smart money in the clubs in Lagos was running five to one against the Yanks making it. Many people didn't think they would ever be seen again; reports had come in that the Glovers, a British couple touring the area the Americans hoped to cross, had been murdered by desert brigands.

Not too far out of Lagos the real Africa closed in. The Americans chopped their way through the bush and half carried the Triumphs through places in heat that might have killed them but for their youth. Dugout canoes ferried the naive adventurers and their bikes across rivers. They camped where night caught up with them, and they listened as drums thumped rhythmically through the forests. Wilson plucked his banjo and the boys serenaded the locals with "Show Me The Way To Go Home," which turned out to be the marching song of the expedition.

English colonial types and French soldiers were dumbfounded when the Americans rolled out of the west, out of a wilderness thought impassable except by foot, horse, or camel. The Americans were assured at each post they came to that the country to the east would be impossible for them to cross. They struggled on anyway. Sand ground away at the faithful Triumphs. Water holes were often seventy-five to a hundred miles apart. Once, desperate for water, Wilson tracked a hyena through the gathering dusk to a scummy water hole. Another hyena lay dead, bloated and stinking in the water. Wilson pushed the putrid carcass aside and filled his canteen. Either that or die.

They followed footpaths and caravan trails. Lonely French soldiers, delighted by the unexpected diversion, gave the Yanks all the assistance they could. Only one person they met during the entire trip told them they would succeed, a Frenchman who said, "The world is full of people who would make cowards of one."

At one desert outpost the local sultan had girls dancing for them from dawn to dusk, and when it came time for them to leave, a volley was fired from three hundred rifles while hundreds of tribesmen thundered by on camels and horses. It's hard to find hospitality or a sendoff like that these days . . .

Francis Flood had never been on a motorcycle until he got to Africa, nor was he mechanically inclined. Wilson, on the other hand, was a biker from way back, and a farm boy who had learned to create mechanical marvels with baling wire and a pair of pliers; it was he who kept the Triumphs thumping along. The book he wrote about their trip, *Three-Wheeling Through Africa*, reads like the nightmare diary of a mechanical genius. When a spring broke, he made a forge out of a gas can, Flood providing the draft by puffing through a dismounted handlebar. A breaker bearing was fashioned from the hard rubber of Flood's dental plate. A wrist pin bushing was replaced by filing to fit a piece of brass tubing salvaged at a French fort. The bikes were dismantled many times in order to grind valves and to scoop sand out of the machinery.

Local villagers who had never seen a motor vehicle, and many who had never seen white men, ran away when they caught sight of the noisy machines and their ragged riders. Flood and Wilson would have to coax the people back into town so that they could get food. In one remote village the boys came upon the Glovers, who had, after all, survived the gun battle in the desert. The English couple and the Yank bikers shared skimpy rations.

Flood and Wilson were able to buy enough gasoline at the occasional European fort or outpost. When they got to Khartoum, Flood was treated for some broken bones in a foot, an injury he had suffered in a fall . . . about twelve hundred miles back in the bush. His dental plate was repaired, too.

Across the Nile and into Italian Eritrea. Then one day the Red Sea hills above Massawah, Eritrea, echoed to the pop-pop-popping of two tired Triumphs. The battered bikes and their gaunt riders rolled down the hills in the warm sun, down to the sea. Behind them lay 3,800 miles of jungle, desert, swamp. James Wilson and Francis Flood had done it, crossed the continent by motorcycle. Smart money back in Lagos had failed to take into account the determination of the two young Americans and the incredible toughness of the Triumphs.

Wilson was right, it was a hell of a stunt. As he says in his book, "any fool can step on the starter and drive a car, but motorbiking is an art—especially motorbiking across Africa!"

Wilson's book has been out of print for decades. The publisher, The Bobbs-Merrill Company, tells us that James Wilson is dead. The Flood-Wilson trip is virtually forgotten. Too bad. What an interesting story it is. Six months in the African bush with a motorcycle. Good sport.

* * *

ALMOST THIRTY YEARS had passed between Dr. Horatio Jackson's trek and the jaunt across Africa by Flood and Wilson. In 1932, when Flood and Wilson bounced down to the Red Sea, they could have ridden a motorcycle all the way across the United States in six days. Motor travel in the United States had become almost as easy as . . . as . . . train travel.

Americans had won their freedom from the railroad,

Francis Flood, left, and James Wilson mounted on one of their Triumphs. They called their bikes Rough and Tumble. This scene is probably in the Sudan, after the boys had survived the hardest part of the first crossing of Africa by motorcycle.
Francis Flood/James Wilson

and, for the most part, we were glad of it. Progress. In the 1930s the eventual cost of our freedom was not yet apparent, and would not become totally apparent to almost everybody until the 1970s, when one day we woke up to discover we were no longer entirely in control of our own destiny. All at once the gasoline powered automobile had become a double-edged sword in our economic armory. A once fairly self-sufficient country, the United States was now dependent on a precarious supply of most of our oil from mercurial peoples whose only allegiance to us is caused by an apparent desire to corner all of the dollars in the world.

The automobile has lost most of its original charm. But we're stuck with it. Without our annual glut of cars, we would be plunged into the deepest of depressions. An economic merry-go-round. And many of our cities are laid out so that they have become a dangerous wilderness for the pedestrian. Such cities have become ugly, polluted, built for automobiles, not human beings.

Way back when, we seemed to have a good reason to abandon the trains. Good Americans, we expressed our latent desire to get out on our own into the midst of our beautiful country. Motoring was an alternative to taking the train.

Too bad, too bad it still isn't that, a true alternative. Train travel is so *relaxing*. Lost in an anonymous security of the train, all responsibility surrendered to the engineers, porters, waiters, conductors, and brakemen. Most of the world and its cares were left behind someplace, unable to catch up. Just watch the farms and prairie pass. Mountains and rivers. Telegraph lines looping down and up, down and up. Mesmerizing.

Tracks disappearing into infinity behind the club car. You are lost in time and space, not able to do much about your existence even if you want to.

In any event, the automobile as we now know it is something of an overly complicated anachronism. Electric cars can be developed for town use. This doesn't necessarily eliminate pollution because the electricity has to be produced someplace, but the polluting effects of electrical plants can be better controlled than millions of privately-owned, worn-out gasoline cars. Electric cars now have the capacity to make at least moderately long runs into the hinterland.

Very possibly steam cars could be revived for those citizens who need a more powerful vehicle. Compared to gasoline cars, steamers are simplicity itself. Although they do need fuel to get up steam, the fuel can be of a quality inferior to gasoline, thereby allowing us to get more miles out of a barrel of crude. Virtually all of the complaints the original drivers had against steamers were satisfied by the 1930s. Steamers are simple, quiet, smooth in acceleration, very possibly a machine of the future. The true capabilities of the steamers were never fully realized during their heyday.

The pioneer days of motoring, more or less the period between 1900 and 1930, are an interesting study for those of us who would try to make sense out of where we are now and where we are going with our automobile-dominated society. There seems to have been a sense of excitement about the notion of hopping into your very own machine and heading out over the horizon, a sense of adventure generally lost from motoring now.

Yes, that's what it was. Adventure.

This 1929 Lincoln roadster has resided in New Mexico since it was new. At first, it was owned by a wealthy family in Albuquerque, then an artist in Santa Fe. It is now owned by a Santa Fe merchant. It would have cost about $5,000 when it was new. This is a fine example of a classic American automobile. Engine: 384 cid V-8. Wheelbase: 136 inches. Special compartment for golf clubs. Leather luggage compartment behind rumble seat. A jaunt in its rumble seat is a vintage thrill. When the present owner was still in school he used to see this car rolling around the streets of Albuquerque.
Albert Manchester

One that didn't make it. The car, that is. The author sits in a long-abandoned wreck in the Big Bend country of Texas, in October 1985.
Ann Manchester

Bibliography

Bakker, Elna and Richard G. Lillard. *The Great Southwest.* Palo Alto, California: American West Publishing Company, 1972.

Barrett, William E. *The First War Planes.* Greenwich, Connecticut: Fawcett Books 460. Fawcett Publications, Inc., 1969.

Beck, Warren A. and Ynez D. Haase. *Historical Atlas of New Mexico.* Norman, Oklahoma: University of Oklahoma Press, 1969.

Belasco, Warren James. *Americans On The Road.* Cambridge, Massachusetts: The MIT Press, 1979.

Bentley, John. *Great American Automobiles.* Englewood Cliffs, New Jersey: Prentice Hall, Inc., 1957.

Blumenson, Martin. *The Patton Papers 1885-1940.* Boston: Houghton Mifflin Company, 1972.

Clendenen, Clarence C. *Blood On The Border.* Toronto, Ontario: The MacMillan Company, Collier-MacMillan, Ltd., 1969.

Clymer, Floyd. *Steam Car Scrapbook.* New York: Bonanza Books, 1955.

Cooke, Alistair. *Alistair Cooke's America.* New York: Alfred A. Knopf, 1973.

Cowles, Virginia. *1919 An End And A Beginning.* New York: Harper & Row Publishers, 1967.

Dixon, Winifred Hawkridge. *Westward Hoboes.* New York: Charles Scribner's Sons, 1922.

Eisenhower, Dwight D. *At Ease.* Garden City, New York: Doubleday & Company, Inc., 1967.

Engleman's Autocraft. New York: Chilton Book Company, 1970.

Fetler, John. *Pikes Peak People.* New York: Ballentine Books, 1966.

Finger, Charles J. *Foot-Loose In The West.* New York: William Morrow and Company, 1932.

Gannett, Lewis. *Sweet Land.* New York: Doubleday, Doran & Company, Inc., 1934.

Gibbs-Smith, C.H. *Flight Through The Ages.* New York: Thomas J. Crowell Company, Inc., 1974.

Gralton, Virginia. *Mary Colter.* Flagstaff, Arizona: Northland Press, 1980.

Gutkind, Lee. *Bike Fever.* New York: Avon Books, 1973.

Handbook Of Travel. Cambridge, Massachusetts: Prepared By The Harvard Travellers Club, Harvard University Press, 1917.

Hill, Ralph Nading. *The Mad Doctor's Drive.* Brattleboro, Vermont: The Stephen Greene Press, 1964.

Hogner, Dorothy Childs. *Westward, High, Low and Dry.* New York: E.P. Dutton and Company, Inc., 1938.

Jacobin, Louis. *Guide to Alaska.* Juneau, Alaska: Alaska Tourist Guide Co., 1946.

Jakle, John A. *The Tourist.* Lincoln, Nebraska: University of Nebraska Press, 1985.

Jerome, John. *Truck.* New York: Bantam Books, 1977.

Lindbergh, Charles A. *The Spirit of St. Louis.* New York: Charles Scribner's Sons, 1953.

Lummis, Charles F. *The Land Of Poco Tiempo.* Albuquerque: The University of New Mexico Press, 1966.

McComb, F. Wilson. *Veteran Cars.* New York: Hamlyn Publishing Group Limited, 1974.

Murphy, Elizabeth Taft. *It's Good To Remember.* Milwaukee, Wisconsin: Ideals Publishing Corp., 1974.

Musselman, M.M. *Get A Horse!* New York: J.B. Lippincott Company, 1950.

New Mexico—A Guide To The Colorful State. New York: American Guide Series Hastings House. Compiled by Workers of The Writers' Program of the Works Project Administration in the State of New Mexico, 1940.

Nicholson, T.R. *Passenger Cars, 1905-1912.* New York: The MacMillan Company, 1971.

Nicholson, T.R. edited by. *The Motor Book Anthology 1895-1914.* London: Metheun & Co., Ltd., 1962.

Nolan, William F. *Barney Oldfield.* New York: G.P. Putnam's Sons, 1961.

Official Automobile Blue Book. Volume 8, 1915.

Paine, Albert Bigelow. *The Car That Went Abroad.* New York: Harper & Row Publishers, 1921.

Post, Emily. *By Motor To The Golden Gate.* New York: D. Appleton and Company, 1916.

Purdy, Ken. *Bright Wheels Rolling.* Philadelphia: MacRae Smith Company, 1954.

Rae, John B. *The Road And The Car In American Life.* Cambridge, Massachusetts: The MIT Press, 1971.

Rae, John B. *The American Automobile.* Chicago: University of Chicago Press, 1965.

Ritchie, Andrew. *King Of The Road (An Illustrated History Of Cycling).* Berkeley, California: Ten Speed Press, 1975.

Roberts, Peter. *The Automobile.* New York: Bonanza Books, 1978.

Sears, Stephen W. *The Automobile In America.* New York: American Heritage Publishing Co., Inc., 1977.

Silverberg, Robert. *Ghost Towns Of The American West.* New York: Ballantine Books, 1968.

Sloane, Eric. *Return To Taos.* New York: Wilfred Funk, Inc., 1960.

Sprague, Marshall. *Newport In The Rockies.* Chicago: Sage Books, The Swallow Press, Inc., 1961.

Stein, Ralph. *The World Of The Automobile.* New York: Grosset & Dunlap, 1973.

Swarthout, Glendon. *They Came To Cordura.* New York: Signet Book, The New American Library, 1958.

The Vintage Auto Almanac. Bennington, Vermont: Hemmings Motor News, 1978.

The World Of Automobiles. An Illustrated Encyclopedia Of The Motor Car. Volumes 2 and 3. New York: Columbia House, 1974.

This Fabulous Century 1930-1940, Volume IV. New York: Time-Life Books, 1969.

Thomas, Diane H. *The Southwestern Indian Detours.* Phoenix, Arizona: Hunter Publishing Co., 1978.

Tompkins, Frank. *Chasing Villa.* Harrisburg, Pennsylvania: The Military Service Publishing Company, 1934.

Treatt, Stella Court. *Cape To Cairo.* Boston: Little, Brown and Company, 1927.

Vandiver, Frank E. *Black Jack, The Life And Times Of John J. Pershing,* Volume II. College Station: Texas A & M University Press, 1977.

White, E.B. *The Second Tree From The Corner.* New York: Harper & Brothers Publishers, 1935.

Wilson, Arthur R. *Field Artillery Manual, Volume I.* Menasha, Wisconsin: George Banta Publishing Company, 1925.

Wilson, James C. *Three-Wheeling Through Africa.* New York: Bobbs-Merrill Company, 1936.

Woodward, W.E. *The Way Our People Lived.* New York: E.P. Dutton & Company, Inc., 1944.

PAMPHLETS — BROCHURES — PERIODICALS — MAGAZINES

Bauman, Richard. "The Magic Highway." Car Collector and Car Classics, July, 1985.

Crowell-Davis, William. "The Cost of Transcontinental Touring in 1920." Car Collector and Car Classics, February, 1981.

Kaye, Glen. "Trail Ridge." Rocky Mountain Nature Association, 1982.

Manchester, Albert D. "Motorized Pioneers—The Indian Detours." Car Collector and Car Classics, September, 1981.

Manchester, Albert D. "Pierce-Arrows Up Pikes Peak." Car Collector and Car Classics, October, 1982.

Manchester, Albert D. "The Car With The Yellow Spoke Wheels." Car Collector and Car Classics, December, 1982.

Manchester, Albert D. "Wheels Across The Border." Car Collector and Car Classics, June, 1983.

Manchester, Albert D. "Cape To Cairo." Car Collector and Car Classics, September, 1983.

Manchester, Albert D. "North . . . To Alaska?" Car Collector and Car Classics, November, 1983.

Manchester, Albert D. "The Last Road North." Alaska magazine, April, 1984.

Manchester, Albert D. "Biking Into The Klondike." Canadian Biker Magazine, June, 1984.

Manchester, Albert D. "Triumphs Across Africa . . . 1931-1932." Canadian Biker Magazine, October, 1984.

Official military reports of 1919 on file at Dwight D. Eisenhower Library, Abilene, Kansas

Oleksy, Walter. "Cross-Country In 32 Days." Car Collector and Car Classics, July, 1984.

Rand McNally Official Auto Road Atlas of the United States. New York: Rand McNally & Company, 1934.

The Harley-Davidson Story. Wisconsin: Harley-Davidson Motor Company, 1982.

The Koshare Book. Published by The Koshare Tours and The Albuquerque Chamber of Commerce.

The Texaco Star, Vol. II No. 3. New York: Public Relations Archives, Texaco, Inc., January, 1915.

The Texaco Star, Vol. XIII No. 5. New York: Public Relations Archives, Texaco, Inc., May, 1926.

The Texas Dealer. New York: Public Relations Archives, Texaco, Inc., August, 1957.

War Diary. First Aero Squadron, Signal Corps, March 12 to April 23, 1916.

White Trucks In Military Service. Issued for private distribution to officers of the United States Army. Cleveland: The White Company.

Index

* denotes photograph or illustration.

The typeface used in this book is Century Schoolbook, with headings set in Souvenir.

Typesetting: Publisher's Studio, Waukesha, Wisconsin, and Roc-Pacific Typographics, Los Angeles

Color Separations: Jim Walter Graphics, Beloit, Wisconsin

Printing: G. R. Huttner Litho, Burbank, California

Book Design and Layout by Paul Hammond